The History of the Blues

THE MUSIC LIBRARY

The History of the Blues

Michael V. Uschan

LUCENT BOOKS
A part of Gale, Cengage Learning

GALE
CENGAGE Learning

Detroit • New York • San Francisco • New Haven, Conn • Waterville, Maine • London

LIBRARY OF CONGRESS CATALOGING-IN-PUBLICATION DATA

Uschan, Michael V., 1948-
    The history of the blues / by Michael V. Uschan.
        p. cm. -- (The music library)
    Includes bibliographical references and index.
    ISBN 978-1-4205-0929-8 (hardcover)
    1. Blues (Music)--History and criticism. I. Title.
    ML3521.U85 2013
        781.64309--dc23   2012037341

Lucent Books
27500 Drake Rd
Farmington Hills MI 48331

ISBN-13: 978-1-4205-0929-8
ISBN-10: 1-4205-0929-2

Printed in the United States of America
1 2 3 4 5 6 7 17 16 15 14 13

CONTENTS

In the nineteenth century, English novelist Charles Kingsley wrote, "Music speaks straight to our hearts and spirits, to the very core and root of our souls. . . . Music soothes us, stirs us up . . . melts us to tears." As Kingsley stated, music is much more than just a pleasant arrangement of sounds. It is the resonance of emotion, a joyful noise, a human endeavor that can soothe the spirit or excite the soul. Musicians can also imitate the expressive palette of the earth, from the violent fury of a hurricane to the gentle flow of a babbling brook.

The word *music* is derived from the fabled Greek muses, the children of Apollo who ruled the realms of inspiration and imagination. Composers have long called upon the muses for help and insight. Music is not merely the result of emotions and pleasurable sensations, however.

Music is a discipline subject to formal study and analysis. It involves the juxtaposition of creative elements such as rhythm, melody, and harmony with intellectual aspects of composition, theory, and instrumentation. Like painters mixing red, blue, and yellow into thousands of colors, musicians blend these various elements to create classical symphonies, jazz improvisations, country ballads, and rock-and-roll tunes.

Throughout centuries of musical history, individual musical elements have been blended and modified in infinite ways. The resulting sounds may convey a whole range of moods, emotions, reactions, and messages. Music, then, is both an expression and reflection of human experience and emotion.

The foundations of modern musical styles were laid down by the first ancient musicians who used wood, rocks, animal skins—and their own bodies—to re-create the sounds of the natural world in which they lived. With their hands, their feet, and their very breath they ignited the passions of listeners and moved them to their feet. The dancing, in turn, had a mesmerizing and hypnotic effect that allowed people to transcend their worldly concerns. Through music they could achieve a level of shared experience that could not be found in other forms of communication. For this reason, music has always been part of religious endeavors, from ancient Egyptian spiritual ceremonies to modern Christian masses. And it has inspired dance movements from kings and queens spinning the minuet to punk rockers slamming together in a mosh pit.

By examining musical genres ranging from Western classical music to rock and roll, readers will find a new understanding of old music and develop an appreciation for new sounds. Books in Lucent's Music Library focus on the music, the musicians, the instruments, and on music's place in cultural history. The songs and artists examined may be easily found in the CD and sheet music collections of local libraries so that readers may study and enjoy the music covered in the books. Informative sidebars, annotated bibliographies, and complete indexes highlight the text in each volume and provide young readers with many opportunities for further discussion and research.

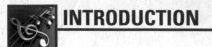

The Heart of the Blues

On February 21, 2010, the blues came to the White House. U.S. president Barack Obama hosted a prestigious concert that featured blues artists B.B. King, Buddy Guy, Jeff Beck, Mick Jagger, Susan Tedeschi, and Shemekia Copeland. King, one of the finest blues guitarists of all time, kicked off the musical event with a rousing performance of "Let the Good Times Roll" and "The Thrill Is Gone," one of his biggest hits. When Jagger, Copeland, and Tedeschi combined their talents on "Miss You," the president and First Lady Michelle Obama stood and clapped to the song's bouncing rhythm.

The concert ended with "Sweet Home Chicago," which blues legend Robert Johnson wrote and recorded in the 1930s. The assembled artists joined in to sing the blues standard that is a musical tribute to Chicago, Illinois, where Obama lived before being elected president. Guy asked the president to join the all-star ensemble, and Obama delighted performers by crooning a few lines. Jagger handed the president the microphone, and he twice sang in a low voice, "Come on . . . baby don't you want to go." The president then passed the microphone to King but got it back again to end the song with a final "Sweet Home Chicago."[1] Obama's surprisingly soulful performance generated newspaper and television stories as well as YouTube videos.

The gathering was part of the White House celebration of Black History Month. African Americans created the blues and have been the genre's most illustrious singers and musicians. In remarks before the concert, Obama—the nation's first African American president—explained why the blues are historically important:

> This is music with humble beginnings—roots in slavery and segregation, a society that rarely treated black Americans with the dignity and respect that they deserved. The blues bore witness to these hard times. And like so many of the men and women who sang them, the blues refused to be limited by the circumstances of their birth. [This] music speaks to something universal. No one goes through life without both joy and

Legendary performers including B.B. King, Buddy Guy, and Warren Haynes (left to right) perform at the White House in 2010 at an event saluting the blues.

pain, triumph and sorrow. The blues gets all of that, sometimes with just one lyric or one note.[2]

Obama's remarks summed up why millions of people around the world—of every race and nationality—revere the blues not only as foot-tapping, enjoyable music but also as music that contains deep emotional messages.

An American Music

Revered African American poet James Weldon Johnson wrote in the 1920s that the blues was one of "the only things artistic that have yet sprung from American soil and been universally acknowledged as distinctive American products."[3] Until African American singers and musicians in the late nineteenth century created the blues, Americans had only produced variations of European musical styles ranging from classical compositions to folk songs. The blues was the first distinctly American music because it included rhythms and musical elements derived from African music, such as call and response and blue notes, that were foreign to Western music.

Blues historians also believe that what made the blues such a powerful new form of music was the content of its songs, which express deep and personal emotions such as anger, sadness, bitterness, fear, joy, and triumph. Blues historian Paul Oliver writes about the special quality of this music genre:

> The blues is both a state of mind and a music which gives voice to it. Blues is the wail of the forsaken, the cry of independence, the passion of the lusty, the anger of the frustrated and the laughter of the fatalist. [The] blues is the personal emotion of the individual finding through music a vehicle for self-expression.[4]

The blues appeals to a wide audience because most people understand and have experienced the emotions the songs express. Alberta Hunter was one of the first black recording stars in the 1920s. When asked to define the blues, she replied simply, "The blues? Why the blues are a part of me. When we sing blues, we're singin' out our hearts, we're singin' out our feelings."[5] Lee Conley "Big Bill" Broonzy, a guitarist-singer who was instrumental in shaping modern blues, echoed Hunter when he said,

> ['The] blues is something that's from the heart—I know that, and whensoever you hear fellows singing the blues—I always believed it was a really heart thing, from his heart, you know, and it was expressing his feelings about *how* he felt to the people.[6]

The deep, pervasive current of melancholy that characterizes many blues songs arose from the unfair, often brutal treatment African Americans experienced in the United States. Blues guitarist John "Memphis Slim" Chatman once said, "The blues started from slavery."[7] Slavery in the United States lasted more than two centuries—from when the first Africans arrived in the British colony of Virginia in 1619 until the end of the American Civil War in 1865. After the end of slavery, African Americans suffered institutionalized discrimination and racist treatment for nearly a century.

Despite the sad core at the center of many of its songs, the blues also celebrates happy times that African Americans have experienced. Many blues songs proclaim the sheer joy of living—for example, "Wang Dang Doodle," a tune in which Koko Taylor sings lustily about the big party she and her friends are going to hold that night. And black pride can be heard in "Barbecue Bob" Hicks's 1928 song "I'm So Glad I'm Brown-skin." Many blues songs have celebrated the achievements of African Americans, including "Joe Louis Blues," which honored the heavyweight-boxing champion. In 1959, famed African American writer Richard Wright explained that blues songs often express positive emotions:

> [The blues] are not intrinsically pessimistic; their [often typical] burden of woe and melancholy [includes] an almost exultant affirmation of life, of love, hope. No matter how repressive was the American environment, the Negro never lost faith in or doubted his deeply endemic capacity to live.[8]

Although the blues originated in the United States, people in other countries have expressed similar feelings about life in their own styles of music. In *The Blues: A Very Short Introduction*, Elijah Wald writes that flamenco can be considered Spanish Gypsy blues, *rembetika* Greek blues, *morna*

Cape Verdean blues, tango Argentinean blues, and *enka* Japanese blues, even though the music underlying the songs is different.

"I'm Singing Life"

Etta James, who began singing and writing blues songs when she was a teenager, is one of the most renowned female blues singers of all time. Blues fans around the world mourned James when she died on January 20, 2012. Among them was President Obama, who in his inauguration ball in 2008 danced with his wife Michelle to "At Last," a romantic ballad that was one of James's biggest hits. James was nicknamed the "Matriarch of the Blues" and sung the blues for six decades. She once said she could not understand why anyone would not like the blues, because they reveal so many deep truths about the human condition: "A lot of people think the blues is depressing, but that's not the blues I'm singing. When I'm singing blues, I'm singing life. People that can't stand to listen to the blues, they've got to be phonies."[9]

CHAPTER 1

An African American Music

Antonín Dvořák was a respected European music composer who directed New York City's National Conservatory of Music from 1892 to 1895. During his tenure with the conservatory, Dvořák wrote "Symphony No. 9 in E Minor (From the New World)," which is better known today as the New World Symphony and is one of his most popular works. Dvořák was famed for incorporating folk music from his native Bohemia and other countries into his classical compositions. He did the same thing with music he found in the United States. When his symphony premiered on December 16, 1893, at New York's famed Carnegie Hall, music critics who reviewed his work noted that it contained elements of African American spirituals, a genre of religious music that blacks developed during the slavery era.

One reason Dvořák came to the United States was to discover whether the young nation had been able to create any new forms of music. To his delight, Dvořák found that spirituals and other African American music were original works instead of imitations of styles borrowed from European musical tradition. In a newspaper article in the *New York Herald* on May 21, 1893, Dvořák praised the originality of this music:

I am now satisfied that future music of this country must be founded upon what are called the Negro melodies. This must be the real foundation of any serious and original school of composition to be developed in the United States. [Negro songs] are the folk songs of America and your composers must turn to them; in the Negro melodies of America I discover all that is needed for a great and noble school of music.[10]

Dvořák probably never heard any examples of the blues because in this period they were just beginning to emerge in the South. Yet the blues had that same quality of newness Dvořák admired in spirituals and other black music he heard in the United States. That music sounded original to Dvořák because it incorporated elements of traditional African music that were unknown to European musicians.

Music was one of the few things blacks were able to bring to the United States. For more than two centuries, most of them arrived in the country as slaves. The slaves were not able to bring any possessions from their homeland, but they carried many traditions, such as their music, with them.

Slaves Treasure Their African Musical Traditions

The United States began as a series of thirteen colonies that Great Britain founded in North America. The first colony was Jamestown, begun in 1607 and later christened Virginia. In August 1619, the ship *White Lion* arrived in Jamestown with a cargo of Africans who had been kidnapped from their homelands to be sold as slaves. The Dutch ship traded twenty Africans to the colony for food it needed to continue its voyage. Colonists eagerly purchased those men and women because of a shortage of workers. The number of African slaves increased dramatically over the next two centuries as thousands more were sold into slavery, and slaves already living in North America had children who were automatically considered slaves as well.

Unlike immigrants who willingly came to the colonies, Africans arrived with no possessions except memories and traditions from their homelands. One of the most important traditions for African Americans was music and sing-

Music Helped Slaves

In The Music of Black Americans: A History, *Eileen Southern claims that music and singing helped blacks cope with the mental and emotional agony of slavery. Southern writes that even shouting out field hollers while working was beneficial for them:*

> Music was a primary form of communication for the slaves, just as it had been for their African forebears. Through the medium of song the slaves could comment on their problems and savor the few pleasured allowed them; they could voice their despair and hopes, and assert their humanity in an environment that constantly denied their humanness. As in the African tradition, the songs of the slaves could tell their history and reveal their everyday concerns. [Sometimes] the songs were merely cries in the field—"cornfield hollers," "cotton field hollers," "whoops," or "water calls"—a slave's call or cry could mean any one of a number of things: a call for water, food, or help, a call to let others know where he or she was working, or simply a cry of loneliness, sorrow, or happiness.

Eileen Southern. *The Music of Black Americans: A History.* New York: W.W. Norton, 1997, p. 156.

ing. In his 1940 book *American Negro Songs and Spirituals*, African American music historian John W. Work comments on why music meant so much to the newly arrived slaves: "Music played so important a part in African life that it is natural that the Negro continued his singing after reaching America. The sorrow of his enslavement probably stirred him to sing more than he did before."[11]

Music even helped Africans cope with one of the more grueling aspects of being sold into slavery: the long sea voyage from Africa to the New World. Slaves endured cramped, squalid quarters, seasickness, and a lack of food and water. According to Captain Theodore Canot, an Italian who commanded nineteenth-century slave ships, "during afternoons of serene weather, men, women, girls, and boys are allowed on deck to unite in African melodies which they always enhanced by extemporaneous tom-tom [beating] on the bottom of a tub or tin kettle."[12] Although slaves on other ships were often allowed above deck to get fresh air, Canot also allowed them to play and sing because he knew the music would ease the fear Africans were experiencing about what would happen to them.

Africans bought and sold as slaves in the colonies continued making music because it was an important part of their culture, and because it provided some respite from the toil of their daily lives. In *The Music of Black Americans: A History*, Eileen Southern writes, "The function of music as a communal activity [in Africa], for example, led to the development of slave-song repertoires that provided some

An 1800 painting depicts slaves dancing in front of their wooden cabins while musicians play the banjo and drum. Musical traditions brought from Africa helped slaves cope with their harsh lives.

measure of release from the physical and spiritual brutality of slavery."[13]

Slave music and songs often sounded strange to whites in North America. In 1774, after Nicholas Creswell watched slaves dancing in Maryland to music from a banjo made out of a gourd, he claimed the music sounded "rude and uncultivated."[14] After visiting the South, Englishman George Pinckard also commented negatively about slave music in a book published in 1816:

> They have great amusement in collecting together in groups and singing their favorite African songs; the energy of their action is more remarkable than the harmony of their music. [Their] song was a wild yell devoid of all softness and harmony, and loudly chanted in harsh harmony.[15]

Slave music and songs sounded strange to whites because African music differs in many ways from European music. But it was those African musical elements that black slaves combined with European music to produce the original American music that so excited Dvořák a century later.

Traits of African Music

Instruments such as the banjo were also strange to white Americans. They played stringed instruments such as mandolins and guitars, but the banjo was African in origin. Thomas Jefferson, author of the US Declaration of Independence and the nation's third president, was familiar with the instrument because he owned slaves. In writing about slave life on his Virginia plantation in 1781, Jefferson noted that "the instrument proper to them is the Banjar [banjo], which they brought hither from Africa."[16] Banjos were similar to stringed instruments slaves had played in Africa. The most primitive were made of hollowed-out gourds strung lengthwise with thin strips of dried animal skin attached to a wooden neck. Musical historians speculate that the strings were probably made of heavy material and produced low, deep sounds, unlike the higher-pitched sounds of modern banjos with tighter

African Musical Instruments

In addition to introducing the banjo to the United States, African American slaves made copies of other African musical instruments. Slaves made flutes by hollowing out animal horns and punching holes in them. Although found only in Mississippi, the diddley bow was a long, one-stringed instrument played by beating the string with sticks and changing the pitch by sliding an object up and down its length. Slaves also turned common household objects into musical instruments, such as jugs they blew into and washboards they scratched with wood. Slaves used two traditional African techniques to provide rhythmic accompaniment to their music—they banged dried animal bones together or tapped their heels or feet on hardened earth or wood floors. Slaves often did the latter to accompany a dance called Juba or Pattin' Juba in which dancers patted their chests, arms, cheeks, and legs while stomping the ground. Juba was a form of music in itself, as different slaps on different parts of the body created different tones. Slaves also made drums, but slave owners outlawed drumming because they feared the slaves could use them to communicate with each other as they had in Africa and plan escapes or revolts.

strings. Other musical instruments used by slaves included copies of other African musical instruments such as flutes and household items such as jugs.

Slave music and singing also sounded odd to whites because they used African musical notes and singing techniques. African music employs blue notes that sound off-key to ears attuned to traditional Western or European music. Blue notes, which are central to the blues, consist of notes that are sung or played at a slightly lower pitch than the tones of the European major musical scale. The most common blue notes are the third, fifth, and seventh notes. Singers also employed African singing techniques including guttural sounds, moans, shouts, falsetto, and melisma, a technique in which their voices move between several notes while singing a single syllable. Such techniques are central to the blues and other modern styles of music such as rock and roll, whose development were influenced by the blues.

Southern believes African music differed in one other important way from European music: "Rhythm is the most striking feature of slave music, as is true in all African-derived music."[17] African music, more than European, emphasizes strong rhythms that are carried along powerfully by simple instruments, such as drums, that accent the flow of music. This trait is what makes the blues, and music derived from the blues, such as rock and roll, so powerful and entertaining.

The ngoni—a traditional African instrument originally made out of hollowed-out gourds—was used by slaves in the Americas as the basis for the banjo.

New American Music

Some slaves learned to expertly play traditional European music and instruments such as the piano and fiddle. An advertisement in the June 21, 1748, edition of the *New York Gazette-Post* boasted that a forty-year-old black slave for sale was "well known in town, being a fiddler."[18] Most Southern plantations had slaves or groups of slaves who entertained guests at parties by playing and singing. But at the same time blacks were becoming proficient in the European styles of music, they were also drawing on their African musical heritage to create variations of the music they learned from whites. Blues historian Paul Oliver writes:

> Banjo player and fiddler alike developed techniques on their instruments that were copied by white musicians, but the Negro community was sufficiently separate from them to develop traditions which were distinct. [The uniqueness of this music] suggests that some musical heritage was represented within them which was special to the Negro slave from Africa.[19]

One of those special musical elements is call and response, an African vocal technique in which a lead vocalist sings a line and others echo his words or sing a responsive phrase. Slaves first used this technique in field hollers, songs and chants they sang while clearing fields, harvesting crops, and performing other tasks. Black workers sang field hollers into the twentieth century. Huddie "Lead Belly" Ledbetter, a legendary blues musician of the 1930s and 1940s, recorded one called "Go Down Old Hannah." When the leader shouted, "Go down, Old Hannah," other workers responded with the same words. The leader would then shout "And don't you rise no more!,"[20] and other workers would repeat the phrase. Those simple lines had special meaning to workers—"Old Hannah" meant the sun, and when it went down their work was done.

Rhythmic work songs offered some distraction from hard labor and sometimes helped slaves work in unison as they performed tasks such as digging ditches. The songs sometimes had complicated lyrics and could be about anything happening in their lives. Eddie "Son" House, a revered blues singer and guitar player, was born in Riverton, Mississippi, on March 21, 1902. House heard such songs while growing up and believes they were the earliest form of the blues:

> People keep asking me where the blues started and all I can say is that when I was a boy we always was singing in the fields. Not real singing, you know, just hollerin', but we made up our songs about things that was happening to us at the time, and I think that's where the blues started.[21]

The call and response in field hollers is common to many types of African American music, including spirituals, the first formal music that blacks created.

The African American Spiritual

Spirituals are African American songs that center on Christian beliefs. They are also called sorrow songs because they express the emotional suffering African Americans endured as slaves and their overwhelming desire for freedom, which some slaves believed they would gain only when they died and went to heaven. Slaves were not allowed to attend church services with whites. When they created their own services, their worship practices included African traditions of hand-clapping, shouting, and dancing. When blacks began writing spirituals in the mid-nineteenth century, they incorporated African musical traditions that made the religious songs starkly different from those that whites sang.

African American poet and music historian LeRoi Jones, who later changed his name to Amiri Baraka, claims that "the lyrics, rhythms, and even the harmonies were essentially of African derivation."[22] For example, African call and response can be heard in the well-known spiritual "Swing Low, Sweet Chariot" in which the lead singer sings the title verse several times while others answer by singing, "Coming for to carry me home."[23] And "home," of course, meant heaven. The music that accompanied spirituals was also much livelier and had stronger rhythms than white hymns.

Black Entertainers

When the American Civil War ended slavery in 1865, blacks were finally able to travel wherever they wanted in the United States and had a chance to share their musical talent with even wider audiences. Blacks called songsters, usually men, traveled from town to town to earn a living by singing or playing banjos, guitars, and fiddles. Performing before mostly black audiences, they played and sang many types of music, including spirituals, dance tunes, and popular songs of the day. Many of those songs were ballads like one about the fictional black hero John Henry, who won a contest by outworking a steam-powered machine to dig a tunnel—only to die from his effort.

In addition to individual performers, groups of talented black musicians, singers, comedians, and dancers began touring in variety shows. They played and sang in tents and theaters throughout the nation as more blacks began moving out of the South. The first black road shows date to at

Hidden Meanings in Spirituals

African American spirituals expressed the deep Christian faith slaves developed. These religious songs often centered on the blessed life they could look forward to in heaven after death. Historians believe that lyrics of some spirituals also had hidden meanings that encouraged and aided blacks to try to escape to northern states, where they would be freed from slavery. In *My Bondage and My Freedom*, Frederick Douglass writes, "A keen observer might have detected in our repeated singing of 'O Canaan, Sweet Canaan, I am bound for the land of Canaan' something more than the hope of reaching Heaven. We meant to reach the North and the North was our Canaan." Some spirituals such as "Wade in the Water" contained instructions for runaway slaves to wade in rivers and streams to hide their scent from dogs searching for them. And "Follow the Drinking Gourd" is considered a metaphor for the Big Dipper constellation that includes the North Star, which runaways could use as a compass point to keep traveling north to freedom.

Frederick Douglass. *My Bondage and My Freedom*. New York: Library of America, 1994, p. 128.

JUBILEE SINGERS

MAGGIE PORTER.   E. W. WATKINS.   H. D. ALEXANDER.   F. J. LOUDIN.   THOMAS RUTLING.

NIE JACKSON.   MABEL LEWIS.   ELLA SHEPPARD.   MAGGIE CARNES.   AMERICA W. ROBINSON.

least 1876, and one of the most popular was the Rabbit Foot Minstrels, which began touring in 1900. Blacks also began forming orchestras and choral groups that played various types of music. One of the most historic was the Fisk Jubilee Singers. This student group from Fisk University in Nashville, Tennessee, began touring in 1871 to raise money for the black college.

During the last few decades of the nineteenth century, African Americans had more freedom and opportunities to develop new types of music than ever before. It was during this period that the blues was born in southern states. No one knows, however, exactly when the blues began or who were the first men and women to sing and play it. Music

The Fisk Jubilee Singers toured Europe in the 1870s to raise money for Fisk University, a historically black school in Nashville, Tennessee.

historians have only theories about how the blues came about.

The Early Development of the Blues

Southern believes that the blues evolved out of the varied musical experiences of African American singers and musicians who traveled throughout the South in the decades after slavery ended. She writes:

> The early anonymous singers of the blues often were wanderers, sometimes blind, who carried their plaintive songs from one black community to another, some of them sauntering down the railroad tracks or dropping from freight cars, others coming in with the pack boats, and yet others coming via the dirt road.[24]

These traveling musicians performed in segregated train stations, on street corners, and in black drinking establishments called juke joints. Their songs were usually filled with heartache—an understandable emotion for a people who had only recently been released from the bonds of slavery and who had yet to achieve anything remotely approaching equality with whites. Frederick Douglass, who escaped slavery in 1838 and helped lead the fight to abolish it, once wrote that misery was an integral component of black singing: "It is a great mistake to suppose them happy because they sing. The songs of the slave represent the sorrow, rather than the joys, of his heart; and he is relieved by them, only as an aching heart is relieved by tears."[25]

Music historians believe the blues was a blend of various types of black styles of music including field hollers, spirituals, ballads, and other popular songs. An example historians cite is "Lay This Body Down," a song about dying and going to heaven that men working on boats as well as churchgoers sang during the Civil War. The rhythm of the song helped boat workers labor in unison but also became a religious tune. Southern believes the song could have been classified as a blues tune if the term blues had been in use, because of lyrics such as, "I go to judgment, in the evening of the day; My soul and your soul, will meet on that day."[26]

Southern says the sadness of the words and the hope they expressed for the future, even if it was in the afterlife, fit in with the melancholy mood of blues songs.

Wherever the music developed and whoever first sang it, the blues finally came to the attention of a wider audience in the early twentieth century.

The Blues Emerge

One of the earliest documented references to the blues is from Ferdinand Joseph LaMothe, an early twentieth-century African American pianist, composer, and bandleader who is better known as Jelly Roll Morton. He was born in New Orleans in 1885. In 1902, Morton said that in the city of his birth he heard a woman named Mamie Desdunes play the piano and sing a blues song despite having a disfigured hand: "Two middle fingers of her right hand had been cut off, so she played the blues with only three fingers on her

After the Civil War, juke joints became centers of entertainment and social life for African Americans. This Belle Glade, Florida, establishment was photographed in 1941.

right hand."[27] The song was about a woman standing on a street corner in the rain begging for money so she could feed the man she loved. "This is the first blues I no doubt heard in my life,"[28] Morton said. The theme of sacrificing for someone they love is one of the classic themes of blues singers.

Ma Rainey, who became known as the "Mother of the Blues," began recording blues songs in the 1920s. But she was introduced to this music in 1902 while touring with the Rabbit Foot Minstrels in a small town in Missouri. In an interview years later with African American music historian John W. Work,

Rainey said she heard a girl singing a strange-sounding song about a man she loved who had left her. In his classic 1940 book *American Negro Songs and Spirituals*, Work describes how deeply the song affected Rainey:

> Ma Rainey became so interested that she learned the song from the visitor and used it soon afterwards in her act as an encore. The song elicited such response from the audiences that it won a special place in her act. Many times she was asked what kind of song it was, and one day she replied, in a moment of inspiration. "It's the Blues."[29]

Ma Rainey, seen here with her Georgia Jazz Band around 1925, is considered the "Mother of the Blues."

It was a year later that W.C. (William Christopher) Handy, who is known as the "Father of the Blues," first heard the music that would change his life. Handy was a formally trained musician who had taught music at Alabama Agricultural and Mechanical College for Negroes—today called Alabama Agricultural and Mechanical (A&M) University. He also led several touring orchestras, including Mahara's Colored Minstrels. Handy wrote in his 1941 autobiography that he was waiting in a train station in Tutwiler, Mississippi, in 1903 when a raggedly dressed man with torn shoes began playing a guitar and singing a song that was like nothing he had ever heard before. This is how Handy described his introduction to the blues:

> A lean, loose-jointed Negro had commenced plunking a guitar beside me. [His] face had on it some of the sadness of the ages. As he played, he pressed a knife on the strings of the guitar in a manner popularized by Hawaiian guitarists who used steel bars. The effect was unforgettable. His song, too, struck me instantly. "Goin' where the Southern cross' the Dog." The singer repeated the line three times, accompanying himself on the guitar with the weirdest music I had ever heard. The tune stayed in my mind.[30]

The song had several classic blues elements, including repeated opening lines and a theme about traveling—"Southern" and "Dog" referred to train lines whose tracks crossed. Although the strange music deeply affected Handy, he did not begin incorporating blues songs into his shows for two more years because he thought the music was too primitive and raw to be widely popular. But when Handy finally began writing and performing classic blues songs such as "The St. Louis Blues," he became wildly successful, and his role in popularizing the blues outside the South made him one of the most prominent figures in the early history of the blues.

The Blues Make Life "Bearable"

That the blues became popular once they emerged is not hard to understand for musical historians. Southern believes that people enjoy the blues because they can all understand the music's universal subject matter: "By singing about their misery, blues singers achieve a kind of catharsis and life becomes bearable again. [When] others do listen to the blues singer, they frequently find that they have shared experiences in one way or another."[31]

CHAPTER 2

The Blues Evolve

People around the world love the blues, but the songs they listen to are far different from the blues African Americans began singing more than a century ago in rural areas of the South. The singing style, instrumental accompaniment, and structure of those first blues songs were much simpler and less sophisticated than blues today. Those original blues are known today as country blues or folk blues. Paul Oliver explains what those original blues songs were like:

> When the blues took shape somewhere around the turn of the twentieth century, it had the shouted declarations of the field holler and the twelve-bar, three-line structure of the later [blues songs]. It was a music with an emphasis on invention and expression, and the habit of repeating the first line and rhyming with the third.[32]

The original blues were usually sung to the accompaniment of a lone acoustic wooden guitar. Today, amplified electric guitars that can make musical notes reverberate to produce unique wailing sounds have lifted guitar playing to new heights of creativity. In addition, modern blues songs are often accompanied by other guitars, drums, and wind instruments such as saxophones or trumpets. Blues singing styles today are also more refined than the harsh, guttural tones that can be heard on recordings that legendary blues singers such as Robert Johnson, Eddie "Son" House, and Huddie "Lead Belly" Ledbetter made in the early twentieth century. The form of the songs themselves has also grown more complex from the simplistic three-line verses that were the hallmark of the first blues.

What has not changed is the emotional content of the blues and the direct, personal way in which singers communicate the human experience with their audiences. Blues historian Paul Garon explains that blues singers' ability to share their experiences and express their feelings is still one of the biggest reasons why the music is popular:

> The blues is indeed a self-centered music, highly personalized, wherein the effects of everyday life are recounted in terms of the singers' reactions [to life]. The unique personal level of this presentation [of how the singer feels] is well known for its capacity to present us with the most *uncluttered* descriptions of human life [in any type of music].[33]

The Original Blues

The first blues songs that were created, sung, and played by African Americans living in the South had several distinctive qualities, some of which can still be heard in blues songs today. The songs usually had a four-four time signature, which means that each measure of music contained four quarter notes and each verse of the songs was twelve bars of music long. Those original blues songs were most commonly played on guitars, banjos, harmonicas, and jugs—inexpensive instruments that were easy to learn to play. Blues historian Dick Weissman explains that the stylized lyrics also made the blues a new and unique style of music:

> The lyrics will be in AAB form, which means that the first line of the song will be repeated, with the third line acting as a sort of answer to the previous repeated lines. The end of lines one and two typically rhymes with the end of line three.[34]

An example is the opening of "St. Louis Blues," written by W.C. (William Christopher) Handy: "I hate to see that evening sun go down, I hate to see that evening sun go down, 'Cause my lovin' baby done left this town."[35] The most common themes in early blues songs were about lost love, broken friendships, poverty, and racist treatment by whites. One reason blues songs became popular and remain popular today is that listeners often identify with the singer, or can sympathize with the sadness, bitterness, loneliness, and sometimes hatred that the singer expresses.

W.C. Handy is known as the "father of the blues."

How Call and Response Works

Elijah Wald explains how vocals and instrumental accompaniment work together in call-response in blues songs:

The twelve-bar blues is ideally suited to the West African tradition of call-and-response, in which a lead voice or instrument states a phrase that is answered by other voices or players. In the most common twelve-bar song pattern, the leader sings two repeated lines, each of which is answered by an instrumental phrase, then a rhyming third line that is answered by a final instrumental passage. The Bessie Smith-Louis Armstrong duet of "St. Louis Blues" is a classic example of this sort of musical conversation:

Smith begins by singing: *"I hate to see the evening sun go down."*

Armstrong echoes her final note on his cornet and added a relaxed melodic response.

Smith repeats, *"I hate to see the evening sun go down."*

Armstrong plays a series of slow, drawn-out notes.

Smith completes the thought: *"It makes me think I'm on my last go 'round."*

And Armstrong builds an arching obbligato leading into the next verse.

Elijah Wald. *The Blues: A Very Short Introduction*. New York: Oxford University Press, 2010, p. 4.

Blues songs are, in effect, oral histories of the people who sing them. In that respect, blues singers were similar to griots, African oral historians who memorized stories about historic and cultural events that had deep meaning to people in their tribes or clans. After the 1927 Mississippi River flood—which killed hundreds of people and left about six hundred thousand homeless—blues singers such as "Blind" Lemon Jefferson acted as griots by writing and singing songs about the disaster. In "Rising High Water Blues," Jefferson sings about the tragedy of losing a home: "People, since its raining, it has been for nights and days; People, since its raining, has been for nights and days; Thousands people stands on the hill, looking down were they used to stay."[36] And when Charley Patton in "High Water Everywhere" sings, "I would go to the hilly country, but they got me barred,"[37] he was referring to the way whites treated blacks during the flood. They kept them from fleeing to higher ground and made them labor to save white homes from the rising waters or clean up flood damage.

Jefferson and other early country blues stars sang more crudely than blues singers today. Eileen Southern describes the way they sounded: "The voice quality was strained, raspy, abrasive, nasal, fierce; there was a great deal of falsetto, humming, growling—whatever it took to sing the lament or tell the story."[38] Yet those raw, primitive vocals were imbued with powerful emotions that often make those songs, which were usually accompanied by only a lone acoustic guitar, more interesting than today's sophisticated blues tunes.

The style of those original blues songs was developed in rural areas of the South. However, the first blues that most people in the United States heard was far different.

The Blues Spread Across the Nation

The blues began to emerge on the national stage in 1912 when the first three blues songs were published as sheet music, which allowed people to learn to play and appreciate them. One was "Memphis Blues" by Handy, who did more than anyone in the early years of the blues to help spread the music across the nation.

Handy had been slow to accept the blues as a legitimate new music in 1903 after he heard an unknown man sing a blues song in a train station in Tutwiler, Mississippi. But when Handy realized several years later how many people liked the blues, he began writing blues songs for his band. In 1914 Handy wrote "St. Louis Blues," his most famous work. Handy's song was in the twelve-bar format and opened with the three-line format of country blues. When his band performed the song for the first time in Memphis, Tennessee, he knew he had written a hit: "I saw the lightning strike. The dancers seemed electrified. Something within them came suddenly to life. An instinct that wanted so much to live, to fling its arms and to spread joy, took them by the heels."[39]

"St. Louis Blues" was one of the most popular American songs in the first half of the twentieth century and did more than any other song to help make people aware of the blues. However, Handy's musical style was more complex than that of folk blues. His small band used a variety of musical instruments, including a clarinet. Handy even incorporated a tango rhythm in "St. Louis Blues" because the dance was popular then. He also used elements of ragtime, another style of African American music that was popular from the late 1890s through the end of the 1920s. Ragtime's main musical characteristic is syncopation, in which a song has a variety of alternating rhythms that are referred to as ragged, thus the "ragtime" nickname for such music. Syncopation is common to many types of African American music, including the blues, jazz, ragtime, and more modern styles such as rap.

A new technology that emerged in the late nineteenth century did even more than sheet music to spread the blues to every part of the nation. Although phonograph records had been sold since the 1890s, few had featured African American music. But when companies began issuing blues records in the 1920s, people across the country began buying them. John W. Work explains how records lifted the blues from a regional music to one that people around the nation and eventually the world listened to:

> Until the recent commercialization of the blues by the phonograph companies [these] songs were the creations of nameless individuals who coined them out of experiences fraught with disillusionment, disappointment, and hopelessness. [Now] a new blues may be heard in all sections of the country in the short period of a month or less for the issuing of the record.[40]

The first blues stars were all women. Their songs, however, sounded nothing like the plaintive country blues.

A New Blues

Executives of phonograph companies had been reluctant to issue records by black artists because they believed African Americans were too poor to buy enough of them to make the recordings profitable. That was partially true until large numbers of blacks began moving out of the South to other parts of the nation where they could get better jobs. In what is known as the Great Migration, nearly two million blacks left southern states from 1910 to 1930. Many of them settled in big cities such as Chicago, Illinois; Detroit, Michigan; and

Mamie Smith, seen here with Willie "The Lion" Smith and her Jazz Hounds in 1920, was the first nationally known blues star.

New York, New York. Blacks left the South to escape segregation and Jim Crow laws that denied them their civil rights and limited them mainly to menial jobs that kept them in poverty. Outside the South, most blacks had more money to spend on entertainment because they were able to get better-paying jobs.

Perry Bradford was an African American pianist, singer, and composer who grew up in Atlanta, Georgia, and performed in many cities before settling in New York. Bradford and Handy battled with record companies for several years to give black entertainers a chance to make records. On February 14, 1920, Okeh Records recorded Mamie Smith singing the non-blues songs "That Thing Called Love" and "You Can't Keep a Good Man Down." After her record sold ten thousand copies, the record company let Smith record "Crazy Blues" on August 10, 1920. Huge sales for the record—in just one month people bought 75,000 copies at $1 each, a significant amount of money in that period—ignited a blues craze in which women were the first nationally known blues stars.

Like other black singers of her era, Smith had sung songs in many styles during a career in which she performed in theaters and traveling tent shows. In addition to singing blues, Smith had also sung jazz songs. Jazz was African American music that developed in the early twentieth century. Although jazz is a direct descendant of the blues, it is more complex musically and is played with a variety of instruments. In describing the sound that became known as classic blues or city blues, blues historian Arnold Shaw writes, "Their blues had a beat. It was blues wedded to jazz."[41]

The women who recorded blues songs were familiar with ragtime, jazz, and other musical styles, as were the musicians who accompanied them. Unlike country blues, which was usually sung by solo guitarists, Smith was accompanied by five musicians who played piano, trumpet, trombone, clarinet, and violin. In *Black Pearls: Blues Queens of the 1920s*, Daphne Duval Harrison writes:

> [Women singers] moved away from the country style and developed a sophisticated, flexible blues styles that could handle the tough but slick sounds that city

listeners were accustomed to. Yet, they employed the husky, throaty pathos, moans and groans that appealed to [both] urban and rural blues listeners alike. This style—the city blues—grasped the issues of urban violence and neglect and rendered them in shouting, wailing, aggressive tempos and shadings.[42]

Other stars of the classic blues era include Ma Rainey, Alberta Hunter, Ida Cox, Victoria Spivey, Sippie Wallace, and Bessie Smith,—who in 1923 earned the title "Empress of the Blues" for selling 750,000 copies of "Downhearted Blues." The song themes fit the generally woeful tone of the blues, such as unrequited love and bad relationships, but also commented on urban problems blacks were encountering, such as drug abuse. Many blues songs also centered on the homesickness and alienation many blacks felt after moving to nearly all-white cities outside the South.

Female singers dominated the blues for the first half of the 1920s. But in the second half of that decade, record companies began recording male singers who played traditional country blues.

Male Blues Stars

The nostalgia urban blacks had for music from the South was one reason record companies began recording male blues singers in 1926. However, historian Angela Y. Davis claims that record executives also began using men because they could pay them less than women singers who were performing before large audiences in theaters and tent shows. In a book about female blues singers, Davis writes:

[It] became an era of widespread exploitation of black men blues singers, who were sought out aggressively by profit-hungry recording companies that paid them paltry sums for their recorded performances, some of which continue to be published on compact discs today.[43]

Some of the top bluesmen in the 1920s and 1930s were "Blind" Lemon Jefferson, "Papa" Charlie Jackson, Charley Patton, Lonnie Johnson, Eddie "Son" House, Huddie "Lead Belly" Ledbetter, and Robert Johnson. Most of them had

Cordially Yours
Blind Lemon Jefferson

been making a bare living while playing in small bars, at social gatherings, and on street corners for handouts. When companies began hiring them to make records, they jumped at the chance even though some received as little as $5 per song. As was common in that period, they signed away their rights to songs they had written, which meant that record companies got all future royalties from the songs. Many of their songs are included today on historic blues collections that sell millions of copies.

Jefferson, the first male singer to become a star, was born blind in Coutchman, Texas, in 1893. Until Jefferson began making records, he had performed in southern cities such as Dallas, walking the streets for hours to earn tips. His first big hit, recorded in March 1926, was "Got the Blues." Jefferson wrote most of his songs and his lyrics included poetic verses such as this one from "Got the Blues": "I got up this morning, the blues all around my bed; Went in to eat my breakfast, and the blues all in my bread."[44] Jefferson was one of several blind singers who became successful recording artists. Another was "Blind" Willie McTell, who once sang "I got the blues so bad, I can feel them in the dark."[45] Oliver explains why there were so many excellent blind singers:

> Blind instrumentalists play a large part in the story of the blues. Unable to make a living handling the plough or the hoe, they frequently resorted to music, with an extra sensibility from their deprivation of another sense and with the time in which to practice frequently making them among the foremost of singers.[46]

Jefferson had a rough, high-pitched voice. Like other country blues artists, Jefferson played acoustic guitar and had no backup musicians. That did not mean, however, that his music was boring. Blues historian Robert Palmer describes Jefferson's unique style:

> On his records, Jefferson would often start off playing a rocking rhythm, only to stop playing at the end of a

---

"Blind" Lemon Jefferson was the first male blues star at a time when female performers were more popular and were paid much more than men.

vocal line, hammer on the strings in imitation of what he'd just sung, and then plunged back in with a snappy, syncopated [bit of playing]. He was a loose, improvisational, sometimes anarchistic guitarist.[47]

Blues historian Elijah Wald writes that Jefferson and other blues singers often used their guitars to musically complement the lyrics they had just sung, a technique derived from the African musical tradition of call and response that is an important part of many styles of black music. Wald writes, "[This] call and response is typically reconfigured as a conversation between a singer and an instrument, either played by another musician [or] by the singer on [his or her] own piano, guitar, or harmonica."[48] The guitar notes, when played properly, would eerily echo the lyrics.

By the 1930s, female blues singers had mostly been relegated to secondary status compared to men, a position they would never regain despite the various female blues singers who appeared in later decades. And those bluesmen would once again transform the blues by amplifying their guitars and adding backup musicians to make their music even more sophisticated.

Modern Blues

Chicago attracted many African Americans who decided to leave the South. By the late 1930s and early 1940s, Chicago had become a major blues center because blues greats such as Lee Conley "Big Bill" Broonzy and McKinley "Muddy Waters" Morganfield had moved there from the South. During that period, those two bluesmen along with many others helped transform the blues.

In the 1930s, Broonzy and other bluesmen began adding other instruments to their solo guitar playing to provide a richer musical background to their vocals, including drums, pianos, harmonicas, and wind instruments. The new sound Broonzy helped pioneer was dubbed urban blues and made the country blues seem old-fashioned. Dick Weissman explains why changes in the old blues style were necessary:

In the urban room atmosphere, a combo provided musicians a better chance to be heard. Bass players

Bottleneck Guitar Playing

People accustomed to the electronic wailing of amplified guitars may consider acoustic guitars dull. Acoustic blues guitar playing, however, can be just as creative and interesting. For example, the use of slides or bottlenecks on guitar strings to create continuous changes in their pitch and how long they vibrate produces dramatic whining sounds that eerily mimic the human voice. Early blues musicians ran the back of a knife along the strings to produce that effect. Musicians eventually quit using knives when they found better alternatives to producing the unusual sounds, frequently the neck of a glass bottle, which gave the name *bottleneck* to a style of guitar playing that blues musicians still use today. Paul Oliver explains this technique:

> [Some] carried a piece of polished bone to slip over the finger to produce the same effect. Among blues singers a broken bottleneck [cut off] at the break, was often used in this way, while others employed a brass ring. Some guitarists used the technique sparingly but others employed it almost exclusively, and its widespread distribution is indicative of the sound quality favored by [most] blues singers.

Paul Oliver. *The Story of the Blues*. Lebanon, NH: Northeastern University Press, 1997, p. 30.

and drummers also provided a more regular rhythmic pulse, which was a definite improvement from the point of view of a dancer. The earlier country blues singers had played outdoors and in small southern juke joints, and no one had particularly noticed their more casual approach to keeping time.[49]

Muddy Waters moved to Chicago in 1943 from Mississippi and helped originate what is known variously as electric, Chicago, or modern blues. In the 1940s, bluesmen like Muddy added to the blues a second but very important new element when they began amplifying guitars and harmonicas. Muddy was the most important figure in creating this new blues style and once claimed, "I took the old-time music and brought it up to date."[50] The amplification was a continuation of blues musicians' need to upgrade their music in noisy city nightclubs and the ability of electric guitars to produce new, more creative types of sounds.

Despite the new blues sound, Muddy retained traditional parts of country blues, including the singing techniques and subject matter of his songs. However, Muddy scrapped the rigid AAB three-line blues lyric format most singers were still using. Instead, he used rhyming variations in many songs that had an ABAB pattern similar to this:

T-Bone Walker, seen here in a photograph from 1950, was known for being a dramatic showman.

Well, brooks running into the ocean, the ocean, running into the sea; If I don't find my baby, somebody gon' bury me; Yes, minutes seem like hours, and hours seem like days; Seems like my baby, will never stop her low-down ways.[51]

Another electric guitar blues innovator was Aaron Thibeaux "T-Bone" Walker, who grew up in Texas and as a teenager often guided "Blind" Lemon around Dallas while he performed. Around 1940, Walker became the first to record blues songs with an electric guitar. With his deft and innovative playing on hits such as "Mean Old World" and "Stormy Monday," Walker influenced several generations of guitar players in the blues and rock and roll. He was also a dramatic showman who would do the splits and hold the guitar behind his head while playing, innovations that the legendary black musicians Chuck Berry and Jimi Hendrix would later copy.

The Main Ingredient in the Blues

The new style blues that artists created in the 1930s and 1940s is the style of blues heard today around the world. But despite the evolution of the blues in the twentieth century, folklore historian Alan Lomax says that the different styles all share the most important element of the blues: the emotional quality of the songs and the personal feelings expressed in them. Lomax writes:

The blues has always been a state of being as well as a [style of music]. "Lead Belly" once told me, "When you lie down at night, turning from side to side, and you can't be satisfied no way you do, Old Man Blues got you." A hundred years ago only blacks in the Deep South were seized by the blues. Now the whole world begins to know them.[52]

CHAPTER 3

The Fruits of the Blues

The blues was the first original music created in the United States. It was so powerful, innovative, and popular that since its birth in the late nineteenth century it has shaped the development of other types of music and has influenced styles of music that followed it. Music critic and historian Tom Piazza sums up the effect of the blues on American music:

> [It] may be helpful to see the blues as a huge river through the middle of our culture. Almost every notable form of American music in the twentieth century is a city, or a village, along that river. Jazz, rock and roll, rhythm and blues, bluegrass, and even so-called serious or classical music have all drawn strength, power, and refreshment from, and so much of their character from the blues.[53]

Piazza's comment is from a blues history he wrote for *Martin Scorsese Presents the Blues*, a five-CD collection. The CDs were part of a multimedia celebration of the blues in 2003 that included a seven-part PBS television special overseen by Scorsese, an Academy Award–winning film director. The series credits the blues as the creative source that inspired other musical styles such as jazz, rhythm and blues, and rap, as well as country music and rock and roll. Or as African American blues performer and record producer Willie Dixon eloquently once claimed, "The blues are the roots; everything else is the fruits."[54]

The first "fruits" of the blues were other black styles of music.

Jazz Is Born

Ragtime is an African American music style that developed about the same time as the blues—the late nineteenth century—but was very different. Like the blues, ragtime had blue notes and syncopation, which means using different rhythms in songs. Ragtime, however, depended on syncopation so much that its melodies seemed ragged, which is how it got its name. The first ragtime songs were performed with banjos, and later, with pianos. Pianist Scott Joplin wrote "Maple Leaf Rag" and is the most famous ragtime musician and composer. Ragtime's popularity was short-lived, lasting from about 1897 to 1918. The reason for its demise was the advent of a new style of music still popular today: jazz.

Jazz originated in New Orleans, Louisiana, and other southern cities in the early twentieth century and is a synthesis of blues, ragtime, and dance music of the period. Eileen Southern claims that the blues was the most influential music that shaped jazz:

> The most distinctive features of jazz derive directly from the blues [blue notes, syncopation, and polyrhythms]. Jazz is an [instrument] oriented music; its players replace the voice with the instruments, but try to recreate the voice singing style and blue notes. Like the blues [jazz] emphasized individualism. The performer is at the same time the composer, shaping the music into [his] style and form.[55]

Evidence of the profound historical debt jazz owes the blues is evident in the title of the first jazz record the Original Dixieland Jazz Band made in 1917: "Livery Stable Blues." However, jazz is a more complex music than the blues. Jazz is performed by groups of musicians and employs a wider range of instruments than the blues, including cornet, trumpet, saxophone, guitar, banjo, and even tuba.

Jazz and the Blues

In 2003 Eric Clapton, one of the greatest blues and rock guitarists of all time, and jazz great Wynton Marsalis collaborated on the album *Wynton Marsalis and Eric Clapton Play the Blues*. On it, they perform a dozen blues songs in a New Orleans–style jazz. Clapton is a native of England and a member of the Rock and Roll Hall of Fame, and Marsalis is a renowned trumpeter and composer, and the long-time artistic director of the organization Jazz at Lincoln Center in New York, New York. Marsalis said it was easy for them to collaborate on the project because they both love the blues:

> Eric Clapton, he's from England, but he's a part of the blues tradition because that's what he studied, and that's what he wanted to learn how to play. Most of the musicians I've worked with, we come from the same kind of music, which is the blues [so] I don't have to play any different kind of way. The music all comes from the same source, Afro-American music, blues, shuffles, basic beats and things that were put in place between the Civil War and the turn of the century.

Nekesa Mumbi Moody. "Marsalis Says He and Clapton Share Blues Roots." *Deseret News*, September 23, 2011. www.deseretnews.com/article/700181705/Marsalis-says-he-and-Clapton-share-blues-roots.html.

The connection between jazz and the blues can also be seen in crossover work from artists of both genres. Jazz greats such as Louis Armstrong, Duke Ellington, and Charlie Parker all performed blues songs, and blues artists sometimes played or sang jazz. Alonzo "Lonnie" Johnson was a blues recording star of the 1920s and 1930s from New Orleans, where he grew up listening to both jazz and blues. A versatile guitar player, Johnson helped develop the role of the guitar in jazz, and Arnold Shaw writes that he was "the most jazz-oriented of the bluesmen of the thirties."[56] Johnson made recordings with Armstrong, Ellington, and other jazz groups.

Jazz, like the blues, was secular music, but the blues was also important in developing gospel, sacred music that began rocking black churches in the 1930s.

Gospel and Blues: "Joined at the Hip"

Although blacks had been singing sacred songs since the days of slavery, gospel had a more modern and upbeat sound. Like spirituals, gospel lyrics were patterned after the way blacks talked in real life. Their themes not only captured the hopelessness of black life, but the hope, love, and joy that came from their deep faith in God. Gospel is similar to the blues in that it features strong vocals and harmonies and has similar musical elements such as syncopation and call

Lonnie Johnson (center), seen here performing in Chicago in 1941, was the most jazz-oriented of the early blues stars of the 1920s and 1930s and played with many jazz greats.

"Georgia Tom" Dorsey is considered the father of gospel music and wrote some of its best-known songs. He is seen here at the piano with the Whispering Syncopators Orchestra in 1923.

and response. And even though the blues was considered profane and gospel sacred, music historian William Ferris notes that many blues singers also wrote and performed gospel music:

> Blues and sacred music are joined at the hip. Most blues musicians grew up in the church where as children they learned to sing hymns and spirituals. One blues musician told me that if a singer wants to cross over from sacred music to the blues, he simply replaces "my God" with "my baby" and continues singing the same song.[57]

Thomas Andrew Dorsey was already a famous blues pianist nicknamed "Georgia Tom" when he wrote "Take My Hand, Precious Lord" in 1932, one of the most well-known and revered of all gospel songs. Its powerful opening lines are an affirmation that God helps people in times of trouble: "Precious Lord, take my hand, lead me on, let me stand; I am tired, I am weak, I am worn; Through the storm, through the night, lead me on to the light."[58] Dorsey wrote the song in Chicago, Illinois, after his wife Nettie died while giving birth to their son, who also died two days later.

Dorsey also wrote "Peace in the Valley" and is known as the "Father of Black Gospel Music." However, as "Georgia Tom" he wrote and performed about four hundred blues and jazz songs. His most famous secular song is "It's Tight Like That," a blues song that became a sensation in 1928 when it sold seven million copies. Dorsey teamed up with Hudson "Tampa Red" Whittaker on the record, which, like many blues songs, is filled with sexual innuendo. Dorsey once explained why he abandoned the blues for gospel: "I was doing all right by myself, but the voice of God whispered, 'You need to change a little.'"[59]

Other blues stars who sang gospel include Sister Rosetta Tharpe, who sang sacred tunes along with blues, jazz, and popular songs. During World War II, Tharpe recorded songs that were shipped overseas to black soldiers. Among the many blues artists who were influenced by gospel is George "Buddy" Guy, who is ranked thirtieth on *Rolling Stone* magazine's list of the 100 Greatest Guitarists. Guy once explained the musical styles he grew up with: "Three types of music were dominant in Mississippi when I was growing up. Blues usually was sung by blacks and a few whites, country was sung by whites and a few blacks, but everybody sang Gospel."[60]

Guy was born July 30, 1936, in Lettsworth, Louisiana. Another style of music that influenced him while he was growing up is easily the most direct descendant of the blues. It is called rhythm and blues, or R&B.

The Blues and Sacred Music

Blues songs have topics dealing with the seamy side of life, including drinking and sex, while gospel songs center on worshiping God. Yet many blues singers have written and sung sacred music because they grew up listening to it. One example is Thomas A. Dorsey, who was known as "Georgia Tom" while writing and singing blues classics but later helped create gospel music. And 1920s recording star "Blind" Lemon Jefferson also loved and respected sacred music. When Jefferson showed up for a recording session in 1925, he refused to play any blues because it was Sunday. Instead, Jefferson sang two religious songs that were issued under the name of Deacon L.J. Bates. Even though Jefferson was being paid only $10, he said "I couldn't play [the blues] if you give me $200. [My] mother always told me not to play on Sunday for nobody. Today is Sunday."

Quoted in Alex van der Tuuk. *Paramount's Rise and Fall: A History of the Wisconsin Chair Company and its Recording Activities.* Denver: Mainspring, 2003, p. 60.

Mixing Rhythm with the Blues

Until 1949 *Billboard* magazine, the bible of the music industry, classified blues as "race music." But on June 25, 1949, it changed the title to rhythm and blues (R&B) because the old name was demeaning to blacks. The term race music had been used since 1920 when Mamie Smith's "Crazy Blues" sold enough records to make the magazine start tracking record sales of African American artists. The category of race music included other types of black music and R&B also became the magazine's catch-all term for any type of black music.

However, the new term also became the name for a style of music that was born during the 1940s and is still popular today. R&B developed from jump blues, a blues style that big bands like African American band leader Lionel Hampton created. This upbeat style combined elements of blues and jazz with popular music, was played by large bands with many instruments, and had a steady beat that made it perfect for dancing. Shaw writes, "If the blues was trouble music [then] R&B was good-time dance music."[61] R&B kept the danceable rhythm of jump blues but scaled down band members to five or six, including a vocalist or multiple vocalists, electric and bass guitars, drums, piano, and a saxophone or other horn.

R&B had traditional blues elements such as syncopation and call and response but was more complex than the blues. It abandoned the twelve-bar blues structure for eight-, sixteen-, or even thirty-two-bar formats that made it closer to popular music of the 1940s. Blues performers often borrowed lyrics from other songs, but that was never done in R&B. It also had a greater variety of vocal styles than the blues. R&B singer Nat King Cole, for example, had a smooth voice that was more similar to that of popular white singers than many black male singers. But Southern claims R&B singers still sounded like blues singers:

> [In] regard to performance style, rhythm 'n' blues followed in the tradition of urban blues and gospel, with much use of special vocal effects for expressive purposes; melodic, rhythmic, and improvisation and call-and-response between soloists(s) and the group. R&B

lyrics were earthy and realist, and the singers typically wrote their own songs, both music and lyrics.[62]

The leading innovator of R&B was Louis Jordan, one of the biggest black stars of the first half of the twentieth century. Jordan was a versatile singer and musician who worked in blues and jazz and pioneered R&B. He sold so many records from the late 1930s into the early 1950s that he won the nickname "King of the Jukebox." His biggest hit was "Let the Good Times Roll" in 1946, an upbeat song that became symbolic of the euphoria Americans felt about the end of World War II and the nation's booming economy. It also had special meaning for African Americans, who were fighting discrimination and improving their lives.

In songs such as "Hard Lovin' Blues," Jordan used the classic blues AAB lyric format: "Good mornin', blues, Blues, how do you do? Eh, good mornin', blues, Blues, how do you do? I would like to have, just a few words with you."[63]

Louis Jordan (center), seen performing with the Tympany Five in the 1940s, sold so many records that he became known as the "King of the Jukebox."

In other songs such as "Let the Good Times Roll," Jordan based the instrumental introduction and verses on standard blues music progressions, but the lyrics are not in AAB style. Jordan and other R&B composers over time abandoned that format so they could have more freedom in writing lyrics. Their songs were so successful that later blues singers such as B.B. King also began dropping the old blues format because it restricted their creativity.

Part of Jordan's appeal was his humorous approach to songs with lyrics such as "Ain't nobody here but us chickens" and "Is you is or is you ain't my baby."[64] Shaw claims that Jordan exuded so much good-natured, irresistible charm in his records and live performances that he did more than anyone to popularize the new style he helped invent:

> Jordan is the pivotal figure in R&B. [His success] fired the imagination of black artists [and] demonstrated not only that there was a market for black oriented material and black-styled music, but it was a big market, white as well as black.[65]

In the late 1950s and early 1960s, that racially mixed market began listening to a new style of music that evolved from R&B: soul.

Singing from the Soul

In the 1960s, the term soul became a term for the growing pride African Americans had for their heritage as well as the name for a new style of music. Soul has its musical roots in

R&B Attracts Mixed Audiences

Louis Jordan was more responsible than anyone for developing the new rhythm and blues sound of the 1940s. Not many whites listened to straight blues music during that era, but Jordan became so popular that whites began buying his records and attending his live concerts. Jordan explains that he was able to begin performing at venues previously reserved for white musicians including the Oriental Theatre in Chicago, Illinois; the State Theatre in Hartford, Connecticut; and the Riverside Theater in Milwaukee, Wisconsin:

After my records started to sell, we drew mixed audiences to [many] clubs. [I] was trying to do what they told me: straddle the fence. I made just as much money off white people as I did off colored. I could play a white joint this week and a colored next. Any time I played a white theater, my black following was there.

Arnold Shaw. *Honkers and Shouters: The Golden Years of Rhythm and Blues.* New York: Macmillan, 1978, pp. 67–68.

Ray Charles is credited with creating soul music, which appealed to a younger generation in the 1950s and 1960s.

the blues, gospel, and R&B. Paul Oliver explains how soul combined traits of older black music to create a popular new sound:

That the soul trend—the blend of gospel techniques of exaggerated mannerisms and screaming, passionate entreaties with blues instrumental techniques and commercial 'pop' words—was immensely popular with young blacks and whites is undeniable. [It] replaced the blues as music that spoke for the younger generation of blacks, while it drew from blues for part of its expression.[66]

The person most responsible for creating soul music was Ray Charles. He was born in Albany, Georgia, on September 23, 1930, and was completely blind by age seven. The piano-playing singer dabbled in many types of music including blues, jazz, R&B, and gospel before finding his most true voice in soul. Charles explained that his progression to the new style was a long one: "Slowly I began to wean myself and come into my own. Still trying to be my own man, but not about to give up what I already had. I was trying to be accepted as me."[67] The new style Charles was seeking began to come together in two 1954 hits: "I Got A Woman" and "What I Say," his first record to sell a million copies.

The lyrics for "I Got A Woman" start out like a blues tune, with "Well . . . I got a woman, way over town, She's good to me, oh yeah" [68] repeated twice. Charles played the piano and growled out the lyrics in his high-pitched, expressive voice. What set that record apart from "What I Say" was the call and response vocals from his female backup singers nicknamed the Raelettes. The new, more sophisticated R&B sound Charles and other singers created helped to make soul more popular than either R&B or the blues. Soul produced some of the twentieth century's greatest stars, including James Brown, Aretha Franklin, Stevie Wonder, and groups such as the Supremes.

Charles remained a towering figure in soul, R&B, and the blues for several decades. He was even successful in making several albums that drew on the tradition of country music. Although country music is mostly associated with white musicians, its musical ancestry includes the blues.

Country and Western Emerges

One reason African Americans were able to develop their own music was that they were socially separated from whites by slavery and, when it ended, by segregation. But there were so many blacks in the South that there was always some amount of interaction between the two races. And the exposure whites had to the blues influenced the development of country and western.

Country-and-western music was born in the South in the 1920s. Its roots were folk songs, popular music, and the blues. Jimmie Rodgers, who is often called "The Father of Country Music," is proof that the blues played a significant role in developing country and western. Rodgers was born on September 8, 1897, and grew up in Mississippi and Alabama, the heartland in which the blues developed. Rodgers is famous for his "Blue Yodels," thirteen songs he wrote from 1927 until 1933 that are written in the twelve-bar blues format and feature his yodeling. His lyrics often followed the AAB format, as in "Blue Yodel No. 1," in which he sang "'T' for Texas, 'T' for Tennessee; 'T' for Texas, 'T' for Tennessee; 'T' for Thelma, that gal that made a wreck out of me"[69] followed by one of his mournful, drawn-out yodels.

James Houston "Jimmie" Davis, another early country-and-western star, was born on September 11, 1899, in Quitman, Louisiana. His parents were sharecroppers—farmers who rented land and shared crops they grew with the white owners of the land. Many blacks were also sharecroppers, and Davis was exposed to their music through their common livelihoods. Although Davis is most famous for the song "You Are My Sunshine," Davis also recorded blues songs and was often accompanied by Oscar "Buddy" Woods, an African American guitar player. Davis used a broken bottleneck to play slide guitar, which he played on his lap in a style made popular by Hawaiian guitar players. Davis later entered politics and served two terms as governor of Louisiana. Despite the debt he owed to the blues, Davis as a politician supported segregation.

The influence of the blues can also be seen in country and western song themes. Like the blues, they are usually about broken romantic relationships and other unfortunate

Jimmie Rodgers is known as the father of country music and is famous for his "blue yodels."

life events. Music historian Tony Russell explains how the blues shaped country-and-western music:

"[Rodgers's] blue yodels were a foundation upon which countless white country singers built. Their great strength lay in their similarity to, partly in their difference from, black blues. The 12-bar structure was fashionable, easily manipulated and aesthetically satisfying."[70]

The blues continue to influence present-day country and western. Country star Willie Nelson, who was born in Abbott, Texas, on April 30, 1933, says:

Growin' up in Texas, I heard a lot of blues singers—black cotton pickers singin' the blues. I always loved the blues and played a lot of blues. It's so close to country music—so many country songs are three-chord blues.[71]

Nelson is also famous for his work in another style of music that descended from the blues: rock and roll.

Ready to Rock

Bill Haley was born on July 6, 1925, in Highland Park, Michigan. During the 1940s, he sang country and western and billed himself as "Silver Yodeling Bill Haley." During the late 1940s, when he was musical director of radio station WPWA in Chester, Pennsylvania, Haley was exposed to black music and began to think "Why shouldn't a country-and-western group sing rhythm and blues?"[72]

On June 14, 1951, Bill Haley and the Comets recorded the song "Rocket 88," which had been recorded earlier that year as an R&B song by black singer Jackie Brenston and his Delta Cats. Haley's combination of R&B and country elements pioneered rock and roll, as did his later hits such as "Rock Around the Clock" and "See You Later Alligator." Many of the first rock-and-roll hits were also copies of songs recorded first by blacks. No one benefitted more from that musical appropriation than Elvis Presley, perhaps the biggest rock star of all time.

Born on January 8, 1935, in Tupelo, Mississippi, the blues was an important part of Presley's musical background. His first hit in 1954 was "That's All Right, Mama," which had already been recorded by R&B artist Arthur "Big Boy" Crudup. One of Elvis's most famous songs, "Hound Dog," released in 1956, came out three years after Willie Mae "Big Mama" Thornton sang the same song and called a man who had treated her badly a "hound dog." Presley did not bother to change the lyrics even though the term "hound dog" had a masculine connotation.

Another early rock star was Carl Perkins, who was born on April 9, 1932, in Jackson, Tennessee. Perkins began playing blues and country and western, but helped create rock and roll with hits such as "Blue Suede Shoes," a rock standard he wrote and recorded on December 19, 1955. Perkins explained how the blues influenced him:

> All my years I worked in the fields picking cotton with black people. We were the only family sharecroppin' on this one farm. I remember that late in the evening when the sun was getting low, you would hear those wonderful voices start to sing out. The music of those people would be flooding the air after a while. To this day, I can hear that music in my soul, the rhythm, the feeling it gave.[73]

Rock and roll shows its blues roots in its rhythms and its beat. In addition, rock bands are generally the size of R&B bands and include similar instruments, with electric guitars usually providing the most important sounds.

The Blues Effect Continues

The most recent descendant of the blues is another African American style of music: rap and hip hop. Although rap, the primary vocal component of hip hop, is usually spoken instead of sung, there is a long tradition of talking in blues songs and other styles of black music. Rapper Common (Lonnie Rashid Lynn Jr.) is a firm believer in the link between the blues and rap: "It's no doubt that there's a connection. Hip-hop is definitely a child of the blues. And I think you gotta know the roots to really grow."[74] Rap lyrics also fit the mood of the blues: many rap songs criticize the injustices suffered by African Americans and communicate powerful emotions about the good and bad parts of life.

The fact that hip hop is only a few decades old is musical proof that the blues is still affecting popular music today.

CHAPTER 4

Famous Blues Women

On August 10, 1920, Mamie Smith recorded "Crazy Blues" for Okeh Records, an independent record label that produced black music. For millions of people, Smith's record was the first time they ever heard the blues. The song had lyrics similar to those in blues songs today—"I can't sleep at night, I can't eat a bite, 'cause the man I love, he don't treat me right,"[75] she sang. But the music accompanying her strong, penetrating vocals sounded nothing like modern blues.Backing up Smith were the Jazz Hounds, five musicians including a piano player and violinist, who played a mixture of jazz and blues that became known as the classic blues.

The song had phenomenal sales—ten thousand copies the first week it was released, seventy-five thousand in one month, and one million in just a year. Its success assured the future of the blues by making a little-known regional style of music popular nationally. Smith opened the door for more than two hundred female singers to make records in the classic blues style. Alberta Hunter, whose career started in the 1920s, said of Smith, "She made it possible for all of us [women singers]."[76]

Classic blues singers such as Smith, Hunter, and Gertrude "Ma" Rainey influenced female blues stars for decades. One was blues great Koko Taylor, who grew up in Memphis,

Tennessee, listening to their records. Taylor once said those women inspired her illustrious singing career:

> I always said I would like to be like these people I'm hearing on these records. What these women did—like "Ma" Rainey—they was the foundation of the blues. They brought the blues up from slavery up to today.[77]

Classic Blues Stars

Smith was typical of the classic blues singers. Born on May 26, 1883, in Cincinnati, Ohio, Smith began her career as a ten-year-old dancer in a white theater act. She later sang in nightclubs and her repertoire included jazz, blues, and popular white songs. Other classic blues stars such as Rainey and Bessie Smith were also experienced performers who had traveled extensively while singing in tent shows and black theaters.

Women were almost the only blues singers that record companies recorded in the first half of the 1920s, because they wanted experienced entertainers who could sing blues in the jazz style that was popular. Their accompanying music was nothing like the country blues, but the themes of their songs were similar. In *Black Pearls: Blues Queens of the 1920s*, Daphne Duval Harrison writes:

> [Themes] of women's blues lyrics are generally the same as those of the men's—infidelity, alienation, loneliness, despondency, death, poverty, injustice, love, and sex. But women responded to those concerns differently and dealt with certain themes more or less frequently.[78]

The majority of female blues centered on men that either loved them or betrayed them as well as gritty but realistic topics such as domestic violence. In "Black Eye Blues," Rainey sang, "I went down the alley, other night; Nancy and her man, had just had a fight; He beat Miss Nancy 'cross the head."[79] Urban drug and alcohol problems were also classic blues themes. For example, in "Dope Head Blues" Victoria Spivey sang about cocaine addiction. Many of their songs reflected a spirit of independence and women's liberation as they claimed they were better off alone than with a man.

Bessie Smith

Bessie Smith was born April 15, 1894, in Chattanooga, Tennessee. Smith became one of the most popular classic blues performers and helped make the blues more sophisticated with her smooth style. Smith sold so many records with hits such as "Downhearted Blues" and her version of "St. Louis Blues" that she earned the nickname "Empress of the Blues." Daphne Duval Harrison explains why Smith became a star:

> Her keen sense of timing, her expressiveness, and her flawless phrasing. [She] drained each phrase of its substance and bathed each tone with warmth, anger, or pathos. But above all, her naturally fine voice and her uncanny ability to transform any material into a great performance earned her a superb reputation. [Her] blues emanated from the violence and combustibility of the urban experience and its effects on black women. [African American poet] Langston Hughes said that Smith's blues were the essence of "sadness not softened with tears, but hardened with laugher, the absurd, incongruous laugher of a sadness without even a god to appeal to."

Daphne Duval Harrison. *Black Pearls: Blues Queens of the 1920s*. New Brunswick, CT: Rutgers University Press, 1990, pp. 52–53.

Classic blues faded in popularity after just a decade, but historian Francis Davis claims the women who sang them had a tremendous influence on the future of American music: "The women blues [singers] helped to change the course of American pop music, loosening up both its rhythms and [introducing] countless listeners in other parts of the country to the music of the rural South."[80] Perhaps none of them did more to do that than Rainey and Bessie Smith.

Rainey and Bessie

Mamie Smith was nicknamed "Queen of the Blues" and is revered for introducing the blues to the nation. But she was soon outranked by two other women with even more prestigious nicknames: Gertrude "Ma" Rainey became "The Mother of the Blues" and Bessie Smith "The Empress of the Blues."

Rainey was born Gertrude Pridgett on April 26, 1886, in Columbus, Georgia. She began performing at age twelve and in 1904 married Will Rainey, a fellow member of the Rabbit Foot Minstrels, a traveling tent show. Rainey hated her nickname "Ma" and demanded people call her "Madame Rainey." Despite her generally regal bearing, the formal title seemed strange for a short, fat woman with crooked teeth. Even blues pianist Thomas A. "Georgia Tom" Dorsey, who worked with Rainey, admitted she was far from good looking.

What made Rainey a star was her dramatic singing style. Paul Oliver writes, "She had a deep contralto voice and sang with great power and feeling, in broad impressive sweeps of sound."[81] Rainey began incorporating blues into her act in 1902 after hearing an unknown woman sing a blues song. Thus her style was more like original country blues than other classic blues singers. Eileen Southern claims Rainey "forged a link between the rural blues of the South and the sophisticated blues of urban centers."[82]

Bessie Smith was born April 15, 1894, in Chattanooga, Tennessee, and began performing on city streets at age nine. In 1912 she began her professional career as a dancer but later she switched to singing and in 1923 made her first record, "Cemetery Blues." The tall, regal Smith mixed the intensity and rawness of country blues with a sophisticated style on more than one hundred sixty records that included hits such as "Gulf Coast Blues," "Downhearted Blues," "Hateful Blues," and "Preachin' The Blues." Her wonderful voice helped Smith become the most famous black entertainer of her period as well as the highest paid. Tom Piazza describes her vocals:

Bessie Smith was the most famous and highest-paid black entertainer of the 1920s.

Her sound was heavy and powerful, yet full of subtle expressive detail. She had a way of inhabiting the lyrics—even the occasionally inane ones she was called on to record—and investing them with a meaning and commitment beyond anything anyone had heard on records.[83]

Smith's last hit was "Nobody Knows You When You're Down and Out." The song begins with Smith singing about having so much money that she did not care how much she spent. But after losing her fortune she sings, "Nobody knows you when you're down and out; In my pocket not one penny, and my friends I haven't any."[84] Smith recorded the song on May 15, 1929, and its doomsday tone was prophetic in two ways. The stock market crashed in October 1929 and ushered in the Great Depression, the most severe economic downturn in U.S. history. The Depression ended the classic blues era because record companies switched to male blues singers who worked for less money.

That corporate decision ended the only period in which women dominated the blues genre. But that did not mean the end of great female blues singers. One woman survived the Depression because of her masterful guitar playing and ability to sing country blues: Memphis Minnie.

Memphis Minnie

Memphis Minnie began recording in 1926 with her husband "Kansas" Joe McCoy. She quickly became famous with hits such as "When the Levee Breaks," about the great flood of the Mississippi River in 1929, and "Bumble Bee," a 1930 song loaded with sexual innuendo that she co-wrote with McCoy. Minnie was like no other female blues singer at the time. She sang country blues and was a masterful guitar player. Blues great Lee Conley "Big Bill" Broonzy, a contemporary of Minnie's, once said Minnie could "pick a guitar as good as any man . . . make a guitar cry, moan, talk and whistle the blues."[85] In the late 1920s, Minnie

Memphis Minnie recorded many hits with her husband, Kansas Joe McCoy, in the 1920s and 1930s.

Memphis Minnie Plays Electric Guitar

Lizzie "Memphis Minnie" Douglas was different from most female blues singers because she accompanied herself on guitar. She and blues star "Big Bill" Broonzy once went head-to-head in an informal contest in a Chicago, Illinois, bar. The audience liked Minnie's singing and playing better, and she was declared the winner.

Minnie was one of the first women to play electric guitar. Although she never played electric guitar on any of her records, famed African American poet Langston Hughes wrote about an electric guitar performance she gave on December 31, 1942:

> The electric guitar is very loud, science having magnified all its softness away. Minnie's feet in high-heeled shoes keep time to the music of her electric guitar. Her thin legs move like musical pistons. [Her] right hand with the dice ring on it picks out the tune, throbs out the rhythm, beats out the blues. [Her playing blasted out of] the amplifiers like Negro heartbeats mixed with iron and steel. The way Memphis Minnie swings, it sometimes makes folk snap their fingers, women get up and move their bodies, men holler, "Yes!" When they do, Minnie smiles.

Langston Hughes. "Here to Yonder." *The Chicago Defender*, January 9, 1943. www .hobemianrecords.com/memphisminniehomepage.html.

defeated Broonzy in an informal blues battle in a Chicago, Illinois, bar.

Minnie was born Lizzie Douglas in Algiers, Louisiana, on June 3, 1887; her stage name is a combination of Memphis, Tennessee, where she performed for years, and Minnie Mouse, Mickey Mouse's girlfriend. Minnie ran away to Memphis at age thirteen and used her guitar and banjo playing skills as a street performer. In 1916 Minnie joined the Ringling Brothers Circus and for several years toured the South. She eventually returned to Memphis and began performing in nightclubs. She teamed up with McCoy, another guitarist, to write and sing. A scout for a record company discovered them in Memphis.

Minnie moved to Chicago in the 1930s and helped pioneer modern blues. Minnie played acoustic guitar on her records and was one of the first women to play electric guitar. Minnie sang songs in a high, clear voice that conveyed frank amusement at her often-suggestive lyrics. While performing, Minnie usually wore jewelry made of money—a bracelet of silver dollars or earrings with silver dimes. Oliver considers Minnie one of the greatest female blues artists and pioneers: "With a formidable guitar technique she was an outstanding blues personality, and in the opinion of many the finest female blues singer outside the Classic idiom."[86]

Classic blues had almost vanished by the late 1930s, but female stars who were not country music artists like Minnie also became popular. The greatest of them was Billie Holiday, who pioneered a dramatic new singing style.

Lady Sings the Blues

Holiday sang variations of blues songs that were heavily influenced by jazz and popular music. In the 1930s the *Chicago Defender* described her as being "looked upon by the public as one of the few remaining 'Queens of the Blues.'"[87] Holiday introduced new rhythms and harmonies to her songs as well as innovations in phrasing lyrics that made her work more sophisticated than previous singers. Holiday's artistry and ability to convey deep emotions made her one of the early twentieth century's most admired singers. One critic wrote that Holiday had a "magnificent searching, sobbing, exciting voice that whispered along the heart strings when she sang."[88] Blues songs are often about the bad things that can happen to people. Holiday was able to fill her songs with real emotion because she had personally experienced most of the lyrics.

God Bless' The Child

A swing-spiritual based on the authentic proverb
"GOD BLESSED THE CHILD THAT'S GOT HIS OWN"

Words and Music by ARTHUR HERZOG, Jr. and BILLIE HOLIDAY

75¢
In U.S.A.

Edward B. Marks Music Corporation
136 West 52nd Street   New York, N. Y. 10019

Printed in U.S.A.

On April 7, 1915, Holiday was born Eleanora Harris in Philadelphia, Pennsylvania, to a single mother. Her childhood was horrible: she lived in poverty, was raped at age eleven, and three years later she and her alcoholic mother worked as prostitutes in New York. She sang for tips in the brothel, but in 1929, when she was only fourteen, she began singing professionally as Billie Holiday. She took her stage name from actress Billie Dove and Clarence Holiday, a musician she believed was her father.

In just a few years Holiday became a star, singing with bands led by African Americans such as William "Count"

Basie. In the late 1930s, Holiday became the first black singer with a white band, which was led by Artie Shaw. During tours in the South, Holiday was subjected to racism. She was not allowed to eat in restaurants or sleep in hotels where white band members stayed, and whites in the audience often taunted her with racial epithets.

Throughout her career, Holiday had many memorable songs including "God Bless the Child," "Lady Sings the Blues," "Easy Living," and "Strange Fruit," which protested the lynching of blacks in southern states. Holiday was a perfectionist who hated listening to her records because she always found fault with herself. She told one interviewer, "It's always something that you should have done. Or you should have waited here, or you should have phrased [it differently]—well, you know how it is."[89] And in performances Holiday never sang songs the same way twice because she was always trying to make them better. Her artistry inspired great black singers from many musical genres, including Carmen McRae, Ella Fitzgerald, and Aretha Franklin.

Although blues songs were only part of Holiday's repertoire, Angela Y. Davis writes that Holiday's creativity was significant in transforming the blues:

> [Holiday's] music was deeply rooted in the blues tradition. As a jazz musician working primarily with the idiom of white popular song, Holiday used the blues tradition to inject suggestions of perspectives more complicated than those the lyrics themselves contained.[90]

Holiday lived a tormented life even after becoming successful. She suffered drug and alcohol problems and relationships with men who abused her and treated her badly. Holiday died on July 17, 1959, of heart failure and cirrhosis of the liver caused by heavy drinking. Another blues singer who introduced a very different style of music is Sister Rosetta Tharpe. Her life was the opposite of the harsh one Holiday led.

Sister Rosetta Tharpe

Tharpe was born Rosetta Nubin on March 20, 1915, in Cotton Plant, Arkansas. Her mother, Katie Bell Nubin, was an evangelist who traveled the South. By age four Rosetta was performing in her mother's show as "the singing and guitar playing miracle."[91] Tharpe is best known for gospel singing, but she performed that genre of black music like no one ever had before to create a style known as gospel blues. Like Memphis Minnie, Tharpe was a sensational guitarist and electric guitar pioneer. Alfred Miller, musical director of the Washington Temple Church of God in Christ in Brooklyn, New York, describes her playing:

Sister Rosetta Tharpe created a style known as gospel blues.

> She could do runs, she could do sequences, she could do arpeggios, and she could play anything with the guitar. You could say something and she could make the guitar say it. I mean, she could put the guitar behind her and play it; she could sit on the floor and play it, she could lay down and play it.[92]

Although Tharpe sang straight blues tunes such as "I Want a Tall Skinny Papa" and performed at the Cotton Club—a famous night club in the Harlem neighborhood of New York City—her true dedication was to sacred music and God. At a live concert in Europe, Tharpe discussed her faith: "I believe in God. I believe in a divine spirit. And I believe that spirit helps you go along if you believe because I could not have made it [through life] if there wasn't a divine spirit."[93] Although Tharpe sang gospel songs in a powerful, clear voice filled with spiritual conviction and heartfelt emotion, her performances included secular music qualities such as raucous electric guitar and blues-oriented vocals.

Tharpe's most famous song is "Strange Things Happening Every Day," which was heavily influenced by the blues and in 1945 became the first gospel song to also be a pop music hit. She played electric guitar and was accompanied by piano, bass, and drums in a rousing, rhythmic song that music historians consider a precursor of rock and roll. Tharpe once said, "All this new stuff they call rock 'n' roll, why, I've been playing that for years now."[94] Many early rock stars admired Tharpe, including Elvis Presley. Gordon Stoker, a member of Presley's backup group, the Jordanaires, said, "Not only did he dig her guitar picking—that's what he really dug—but he dug her singing, too."[95]

Another singer who had success beyond the blues is Etta James.

Blues to the Bone

When James died at the age of seventy-three on January 20, 2012, in Riverside, California, singer Aretha Franklin praised her as "one of the great soul singers of our generation, an American original."[96] Soul singer-songwriter Marvin Gaye once claimed, "Etta could sing the Sears catalog and make you want to buy every item."[97] In her six-decade career, James had hits in the blues, rhythm and blues, and rock and roll.

James was born Jamesetta Hawkins on January 25, 1938, in Los Angeles, California. Like Holiday, her mother was unwed and a fourteen-year-old prostitute. Like Tharpe, she began singing sacred songs. Raised by foster parents after her mother abandoned her, James by age five could be heard singing on radio station KOWL, which broadcast St. Paul Baptist Church's Sunday services. James had early R&B hits such as "Dance With Me Henry" and "Good Rockin' Daddy" but also sang in other styles. In 1961 James released her first album, *At Last!*, which was also the title of what became her signature song. James co-wrote the

Etta James, seen here around 1965, believed the blues revealed essential truths about people. "When I'm singing blues, I'm singing life," she said.

Nina Simone Fights Racism

Nina Simone was a singer like Billie Holiday, whose sophisticated vocals enabled her to sing in a variety of styles. She was born Eunice Kathleen Waymon on February 21, 1933, in Tryon, North Carolina. Her father was a preacher, and by the age of six she was singing and playing sacred music. Under her stage name—Nina, which is Spanish for "little girl," and Simone, which is taken from a French actress—she had a successful career for two decades before joining the civil rights protests of the 1960s.

Simone attacked racism in several songs she wrote and performed at protests. In 1969, Simone told *Ebony* magazine why she fought:

> [As singers] we're able to say through our art, the things that millions of people can't say. I think that's the function of an artist and, of course, those of us who are lucky leave a legacy so that when we're dead, we also live on. That's people like Billie Holiday and I hope that I will be that lucky, but meanwhile, the function [of my life] is to reflect the times, whatever that might be.

Phyl Garland. "Nina Simone: High Priestess of Soul." *Ebony*, August 1, 1969, p. 158.

song that begins "At last, My love has come along, My lonely days are over, And life is like a song."[98] The song was reminiscent of Holiday, who was her idol. James once said "I saw [Holiday] as a distant goddess, a starlet I couldn't touch, couldn't understand, couldn't even call by the name of Mother."[99]

For the next half-century, James was a star despite personal problems that included heroin addiction in the 1970s and arrests for cashing bad checks, forgery, and possession of drugs. James overcame her personal trials to win six Grammy Awards, including Best Vocal Performance in 1994 for *Mystery Lady*, in which she sang her favorite Holiday songs, and Best Traditional Blues Album for *Blues to the Bone* in 2004. In 1990, a *New York Times* music critic praised her for having "one of the great voices in American popular music, with a huge range, a multiplicity of tones and vast reserves of volume."[100]

A New "Queen of the Blues"

Koko Taylor was born Cora Walton on September 28, 1928, in Memphis. Koko was a nickname she earned as a child because she loved chocolate. When she died on June 3, 2009, in Chicago, Taylor was hailed as "Queen of the Blues" after a four-decade career that made her one of the greatest female blues singers of all time. Taylor once said of her stardom, "It was all kind of like a dream. When I was growing up, I never thought I'd be a singer. I just loved what I was doing."[101] Like many blues singers, Walton began singing gospel in church. Even though her parents banned it, she and her brothers would sing and play the blues. The family was so poor her brothers accompanied her on a harmonica made out of a corncob and a guitar made out of hay-baling wire wrapped around nails on a board.

She moved to Chicago at age eighteen with Robert "Pops" Taylor, who she later married. Taylor began singing in blues clubs in the 1950s but did not begin her recording career until 1965. Her first record was "Wang Dang Doodle," a raucous, joyous song about an upcoming party. Although it had been recorded earlier by Chicago blues great Chester Arthur "Howlin' Wolf" Burnett, Taylor's version was a bigger hit because of her booming vocals. The song ignited a career that lasted until her final performance a month before her death on May 7, 2009, at the Blues Music Awards.

Rolling Stone magazine once called Taylor "the greatest female blues singer of her generation"[102] and her many hits include "I'm A Woman," "Voodoo Woman," "Come to Mama," and "Blues Hotel." Taylor also won numerous

Koko Taylor, seen here performing in 1970, led a quiet life and was not tormented by personal problems as some blues singers were.

awards, including a 1985 Grammy, and was voted into the Blues Hall of Fame.

Unlike some blues singers, Taylor lived quietly and was not tormented by personal problems. When she died, Bruce Iglauer, her former manager, said, "She didn't party. She didn't live a wild life at all. But what she did do that was so much of the essence of the blues is she sang directly from the soul."[103] Taylor once explained what she tried to do when she sang: "My music is designed to help people, it's like a therapy. So many people come up to me after a show and say, 'This or that song of yours, it made my day.'"[104]

Gone but Not Forgotten

When Taylor and James died, the public mourned their deaths. But many female blues singers of the past died in obscurity. An example is Memphis Minnie, who died on August 6, 1973, and was buried quietly at New Hope Baptist Church Cemetery in Walls, Mississippi. On October 13, 1996, blues singer Bonnie Raitt paid for a new headstone to honor Minnie. The grave marker praises Minnie for her contribution to the blues:

> The hundreds of sides Minnie recorded are the perfect material to teach us about the blues. For the blues are at once general, and particular, speaking for millions, but in a highly singular, individual voice. Listening to Minnie's songs we hear her fantasies, her dreams, her desires, but we will hear them as if they were our own.[105]

CHAPTER 5

Famous Blues Men

In the early 1920s, companies finally began recording male country blues artists after years of recording mostly female singers. The sound of their blues was completely different from the classic blues that women introduced to the nation. Compared to the women's smooth, polished vocals, the men's voices were rougher, and their diction was that of uneducated southern blacks. They also peppered their songs with grunts, moans, and other strange sounds. Instead of being backed by small bands playing a jazz style of blues, bluesmen accompanied themselves on acoustic guitars. Tom Piazza writes that the men were so different from the women that for people who heard their records, "It was like discovering a lost continent, or a parallel universe that had been there all along, hidden in plain sight."[106]

Sylvester Weaver became the first male blues artist to make a record when he and blues singer Sara Martin recorded "Longing for Daddy Blues" in New York on October 23, 1923. Two weeks later, Weaver and his slide-guitar soloed on a recording of "Guitar Blues." Charles "Papa Charlie" Jackson became the first male singer to achieve stardom the next year when he recorded "Papa's Lawdy Lawdy Blues" in August 1924 at Paramount Records in Grafton, Wisconsin. Jackson was unusual in that he played a hybrid banjo-guitar—a six-stringed banjo with the neck of a guitar that is

Charley Patton popularized Delta blues and often wrote songs about the mistreatment of blacks.

tuned like a guitar but played by musicians who like the banjo sound.

Record companies began going south to scout new male singers. Record executives believed that African Americans who had left the South to escape racism were homesick and would gladly buy recordings of music they used to hear back home. In 1926 when "Blind" Lemon Jefferson made his first record for Paramount, advertisements described his singing as "real, old-fashioned blues, by a real, old-fashioned singer."[107] Even though Jefferson's blues sounded new to listeners, his songs were the original blues first created in the late nineteenth century by unknown southern black musicians and singers.

The Prototype

Guitars were usually the only instrument in country blues songs. Jefferson, Lonnie Johnson, and Charley Patton became revered musical icons and their guitar styles were copied for decades. Perhaps the most influential early blues star was Patton. He was born on April 28, 1891, in Edwards, Mississippi, and by 1907 was famous throughout the Mississippi Delta area. Paul Oliver claims Patton was the prototypical country blues artist: "Patton lived the life that mythologized the idea of a bluesman. He was a heavy drinker, a carouser, a womanizer, a brawler."[108] Like many early country blues artists Patton had roamed southern states, singing blues and other types of music, performing wherever anyone would pay him.

After a Paramount scout discovered Patton in 1929 on Dockery Farms, a plantation in Sunflower County, Mississippi, Patton began recording hits such as "Mississippi Boweavil Blues" and "Pony Blues." Piazza writes that Patton's songs were standard country blues: "These were much rawer and closer to the rural sound of the field holler than

Howlin' Wolf

Perhaps nobody in blues history lived up to his nickname better than Chester Arthur "Howlin' Wolf" Burnett, whose frenzied guitar playing and fierce vocals were reminiscent of the primal energy of a wolf. Burnett was born on June 10, 1910, on a plantation in White Station, Mississippi. At 6 feet, 6 inches tall (nearly 2 meters) and weighing nearly 300 pounds (136 kilograms), Burnett was a massive, dramatic presence on stage. He did not make a record until 1951, but hits such as "Smokestack Lightin'" and "Red Rooster" as well as his fierce stage performances made him a star until his death in 1976.

When Burnett was inducted into the Rock and Roll Hall of Fame in 1991, *Rolling Stone* magazine wrote:

> [No] singer ever managed to convey the blues' deepest obsessions more fiercely than the raw-throated Chester Burnett—the hulking guitarist and bandleader more popularly (and fittingly) known as the Howlin' Wolf. Wolf's singing embodied a sense of anger and menace [and from the late 1940s to the early 1960s], Wolf defined an aggressive, almost primal blues temper, bristling with pounding rhythms and burning, fuzz-inflected guitar parts.

M. Gilmore and D. Ortiz-Lopez. "Rock and Roll Hall of Fame." *Rolling Stone*, February 7, 1991, p. 46.

Howlin' Wolf—seen here performing in Ann Arbor, Michigan, in 1969—was known for frenzied guitar playing and fierce vocals.

anything that had ever been put on record."[109] Patton was a fine songwriter whose lyrics often commented on social problems affecting blacks. One was "High Sheriff Blues," which criticized racist treatment of blacks by law officials: "Get in trouble at Belzoni [Mississippi], there ain't no use a-screamin' and cryin'; Mister [the law] will take you back to Belzoni jail flyin.'"[110]

Patton is most famous for popularizing Delta blues, a style of country blues that features slide-guitar playing and a more complex song structure. Oliver describes Patton's guitar playing and singing:

> Charley Patton, with a gruff, hoarse voice and an equally rugged guitar style, was the single most influential early Delta bluesman [and created] a brand of blues featuring complex rhythms accented by percussive taps on his guitar, elongated melodies, and a slide guitar technique that cut a path that virtually every [future] Delta bluesman had to acknowledge.[111]

In 2006, when Mississippi began erecting markers for its Mississippi Blues Trail, the first one was placed at Patton's grave in Holly Ridge, Mississippi. Patton died on April 28, 1934, but nearly eight decades later a remastered box set of his recordings, *Screamin' and Hollerin' the Blues*, won three Grammy Awards, including Best Historical Album. Despite his musical contribution to the blues, however, Patton is not the most famous country blues artist. That honor goes to Robert Johnson, a blues singer whose legendary guitar skills and death are shrouded in mystery.

The Mysterious Robert Johnson

Although Johnson recorded only about thirty or so songs in the twenty-seven years he lived—he was born on May 8, 1911, in Hazlehurst, Mississippi, and died on August 16, 1938, in Greenwood, Mississippi—he is the most fabled singer in blues history because of his guitar wizardry and strange death. Johnson is also noted for the sadness and inner torment of his songs, which may have come from his tragic marriage. In 1929 Johnson married sixteen-year-old Virginia Travis; the following April she died while giving birth to their child, who also died. The deaths led Johnson to begin playing the blues.

Johnson tried to learn guitar by watching Patton and Eddie "Son" House. But House remembers that Johnson played poorly before disappearing for almost a year. When Johnson returned, he went to a bar where House was performing and asked if he could play. House kidded him that he was not good enough, but when House allowed him to play he was amazed at Johnson's skill: "So he sat down there and finally got started. And man! He was so good! When he finished all our mouths were standing open. I said, Well, ain't that fast! He's gone now."[112]

No one could understand how Johnson had gotten so good so quickly. Two songs Johnson later wrote and recorded— "Me and the Devil Blues" and "Crossroad Blues"—ignited rumors that Johnson had bargained with the devil for his playing prowess. Many people today claim that the meeting between Johnson and the devil actually took place where Highways 61 and 49 intersect in Clarksdale, Mississippi. It was not learned until years later that during Johnson's absence he went home to Hazlehurst and took lessons from the talented guitarist Ike Zinnerman.

Such tales created an aura of mystery around Johnson, and the songs he wrote and recorded were filled with fears of the supernatural and poetic but spooky images. In "Hellhound On My Trail," Johnson sang "I got to keep movin', I got to keep movin'; Blues fallin' down like hail, blues fallin' down like hail; And the day keeps on worryin' me, there's a hellhound on my trail; Hellhound on my trail, hellhound on my trail."[113] Johnson recorded songs for Vocalion Records in San Antonio and Dallas, Texas, in two sessions in 1937 and 1938. Johnson was paid only a few dollars for each song and continued performing in the South. While playing near Itta Bena, Mississippi, on August 13, 1938, Johnson drank from a bottle of whiskey someone handed him, became sick, and died three days later. It is believed Johnson died from poison, a method of murder known then as the ice curse, but no one knows who may have killed him or why.

Johnson never became rich or famous when he was alive. But when a CD of his complete recordings was issued in

Little Walter

The guitar is the instrument that has most clearly defined the blues for generations. The harmonica, also called the harp, has also been important to the blues because it can creatively express emotions and produce unique sounds.

Marion Walter "Little Walter" Jacobs was born May 1, 1930, in Marksville, Louisiana, and died February 15, 1968, in Chicago. "Little Walter" was the first to amplify the harmonica and in 1952 recorded "Juke," an instrumental that today is considered a blues standard. His brilliant playing elevated the status of the harmonica in blues and rock and roll and influenced generations of harmonica players. Blues historian Bill Dahl writes:

> The fiery harmonica wizard took the humble mouth organ in dazzling amplified directions that were unimaginable prior to his ascendancy. His daring instrumental innovations were so fresh, startling, and ahead of their time [with] a jazz sensibility, soaring and swooping in front of snarling guitars and swinging rhythms perfectly suited to Walter's pioneering flights of fancy.

Vladimir Bogdanov, Chris Woodstra, and Stephen Thomas Erlewine, eds. *All Music Guide to the Blues: The Experts' Guide to the Best Blues Recordings*, second edition. San Francisco: Backbeat, 2003, p. 351.

2009, it sold more than a million copies, and Johnson won a Grammy Award for Best Historical Album. Many blues historians consider Johnson the last great country blues singer because the blues began changing in the 1930s. One of the key innovators of the new sound was Lee Conley "Big Bill" Broonzy.

"Big Bill" Broonzy

Broonzy was born Lee Conley Bradley on June 26, 1903, in Lake Dick, Arkansas, to parents who had been slaves and were sharecroppers; his father's middle name was Broonzy. He enjoyed music as a child and his first instrument was a fiddle made from a cigar box. After fighting two years in Europe during World War I, Broonzy returned to Arkansas in 1919. When a white man saw Broonzy wearing his army uniform, he told him he should "hurry up and get his soldier uniform off and put on some overalls."[114] Racist whites bullied returning soldiers and reminded them they would not be treated with equality despite their service in the U.S. military.

Like many blacks in the first half of the twentieth century, Broonzy left the South in 1920 to escape such racist treatment. Broonzy moved to Chicago, Illinois, where he worked a variety of jobs as a cook, foundry worker, railroad porter, and janitor while pursuing his interest in music. Broonzy learned to play guitar from "Papa Charlie" Jackson and began performing at rent parties blacks held in their homes to raise money; he was paid a few dollars and all the food he could eat.

In 1927, Broonzy recorded his first songs, including "House Rent Stomp." They were in the country blues style Broonzy had grown up with and were not very popular. But in the 1930s and early 1940s, Broonzy, along with many other blues musicians, developed a new style of playing and singing that became known as urban blues. Country blues was usually about the sadness of life and sung in high-pitched, sometimes whining voices, but as blacks moved out of the South, many of their songs became more optimistic because their lives had improved.

An example of the new style was Broonzy's 1935 hit "The Sun Gonna Shine in My Door Someday." As Broonzy explained it, "Young people say you're cryin' when you sing [country blues]. Who wants to cry? Well, back in the early days, what else could black people and bluesmen do but cry?"[115] Blues songs, however, still commented on problems blacks faced. Lyrics in Broonzy's "Black, Brown and White" criticized racism that made it harder for blacks to get jobs: "They says, 'If you was white, should be all right, If you was brown, stick around; But as you's black, hmm brother, get back, get back, get back.'"[116]

"Big Bill" Broonzy moved from the South to Chicago to escape racism and helped develop a style known as urban blues.

The biggest change from country blues was not in song themes but in the way they played and sang. Broonzy picked up guitar techniques from Lonnie Johnson, whose complex playing borrowed from jazz. Blues historian Tony Johnson writes that Broonzy was "an extraordinarily fast and inventive guitarist" as well as a more refined singer than country blues stars such as Robert Johnson: "His timbre was warm and rich, every word was understandable, and he seldom indulged in the whines, cries and half-yodels favored by many of his contemporaries."[117] The urban blues also had a more complex instrumental backup as Broonzy still played guitar but added other musicians. In 1945 his recordings of "Where the Blues Began" included a piano and saxophone player, and "Martha Blues" featured a piano.

Broonzy was perhaps the most important male blues star in Chicago before World War II. But in the late 1940s Muddy Waters and his wailing electric guitar made Broonzy seem old-fashioned and changed the blues forever.

Delta Blues Get Muddy

McKinley "Muddy Waters" Morganfield was born on April 14, 1913, in Jug's Corner, Mississippi. His mother died shortly after he was born. Della Grant, his grandmother, raised him on Stovall Plantation in a wooden shack that today is in the Delta Blues Museum in Clarksdale, Mississippi. His nickname came from playing in and eating mud as a child. Muddy loved music and by age seventeen was playing guitar at parties. Like most Delta blues guitarists, he was influenced by local legends Son House and Robert Johnson.

Muddy was a plantation worker until the pivotal moment in his life on August 31, 1943, when Alan Lomax recorded him for the Library of Congress. Lomax was looking for black singers so that he could record and preserve country blues songs. But when Lomax recorded Muddy, he ignited one of the most memorable careers in blues history. When Muddy heard his record, it made him realize just how good he was:

> When he played back the first song, I sounded just like anybody's records. Man, you don't know how I felt that afternoon when I heard that voice and it was my own voice. I thought, "Man, I can sing." Later on he sent me two copies of the [record, and] I carried that record up [to] the corner and put it on the jukebox. Just played it and played it and said, "I can do it, I can do it."[118]

Muddy moved to Chicago and his career began slowly as he worked odd jobs while playing at parties and in clubs at night. In April 1948, Muddy recorded "I Can't Be Satisfied," the song he had sung for Lomax. Muddy's 1948 version,

however, was far different from the one he had sung seven years earlier for Lomax, because he was now playing electric guitar. The record opens with intricate, whining guitar strokes that nicely complement his deep, soulful voice and represent the unique new sound that amplified guitars brought to the blues. Even though Muddy pioneered that sound, he admitted once that there was a major drawback to electric guitar: "That loud sound would tell everything you were doing. On acoustic you could mess up a lot of stuff and no one would know that you ever missed."[119] But Muddy was so good, he rarely made mistakes. And the record made him a star by selling three thousand copies in just over a day.

Although Muddy helped create the modern sound of the blues, he never tried to depart entirely from the Delta blues style played by House and Johnson. Instead, he claimed he was only trying to create a blues sound that would appeal to modern audiences:

> It was in my head. Nobody ever told me about it. You see, the blues is a tone, a deep tone with a beat. By itself that sound would never have made it in Chicago. I guess I'm one of the first people who was thinking of that sound, learning on that sound and when I got her I found people could get close to that sound.[120]

Dick Weissman believes that Muddy probably influenced the evolution of present-day blues music more than anyone else by making it more lively and danceable. Oliver adds that Muddy excited audiences with his electrifying stage presence:

> [Muddy] sang unhampered [by convention], stamping, hollering, his whole body jerking in sheer physical expression of his blues. He would double up, clench his fist, straighten with a spring like a flick-knife, leap in the air, arch his back and literally punch out his words whilst the perspiration poured down his face and soaked through his clothing.[121]

The new sound Muddy created pushed the blues into the future. B.B. King was one of the future stars who would keep the blues popular into the twenty-first century.

Muddy Waters, seen here performing in 1981, helped create the modern blues sound.

A Blues Boy Makes History

Riley "B.B." King was born on September 16, 1925, on a cotton plantation near Itta Bena, Mississippi. King got his first guitar at age twelve and, like many blues greats, he first began singing and playing gospel. When King was eighteen, he moved to Memphis, Tennessee, and lived briefly with his cousin, blues guitarist Booker T. "Bukka" White. White taught King some fundamentals about playing guitar. His other early influences were "Blind" Lemon Jefferson, Lonnie Johnson, and Aaron Thibeaux "T-Bone" Walker, an early electric guitar pioneer whose most famous song is "Stormy Monday." King said when he first heard that song, "It drove me crazy. I could never believe a sound could be that pretty on an instrument."[122] However, King once said that despite such influences he developed his own personal style because "the blues isn't like painting by numbers or following the dots. The blues [is] something you live."[123]

In 1947 King began performing on radio stations in Arkansas and Memphis, where he was called "Blues Boy"— "B.B." is a shortened form of that nickname. In 1949 King began a seven-decade recording career. He had scores of hits including "Three O'Clock Blues," the song that made him a star in 1951, and "The Thrill Is Gone," his signature song, in 1969. "The Thrill Is Gone" is a slow, twelve-bar blues tune that features lush production including string accompaniment. King earned a 1970 Grammy Award for Best Male R&B Vocal Performance for the song, in which he sings sadly about losing the woman he loves. In a soft, soulful voice filled with emotion, King sings, "The thrill is gone; The thrill is gone away; The thrill is gone baby. The thrill is gone away; You know you done me wrong baby, And you'll be sorry someday."[124]

King's guitar playing has made him one of the greatest blues stars of all time as well as one of the twentieth century's most respected guitarists. *Rolling Stone* magazine ranks King sixth on its list of 100 Greatest Guitarists, and he has influenced scores of stars in blues and rock and roll. Billy Gibbons, guitarist for the iconic rock band ZZ Top, is one of King's admirers: "He plays in shortened bursts, with a richness and robust delivery. And there is a technical dexterity, a cleanly delivered phrasing."[125]

On Lucille, the name King lovingly gives all his guitars, he is able to manipulate notes to create emotions of sadness, joy, or triumph and produce unforgettable wailing sounds. King once explained the sound he was striving for when he began playing guitar:

I wanted to sustain a note like a singer. [By] bending the strings, by trilling my hand—and I have a big left hand—I could achieve something that approximated a vocal vibrato. I could sustain a note. I wanted to connect my guitar to human emotions. By fooling with the feedback between my amplifier and instrument, I started experimenting with sounds that expressed my feelings, whether happy or sad, bouncy or bluesy. I was looking for ways to let my guitar sing.[126]

B.B. King, seen here performing in 2012, is considered one of the greatest guitar players of all time.

John Lee Hooker

John Lee Hooker was born August 2, 1917, in Coahoma County, Mississippi. He died on June 21, 2001, in Los Altos, California, a celebrated musician known for his unique brand of the blues. From his stepfather, William Moore, Hooker learned a stripped-down style of guitar playing that featured a simple yet powerful percussive beat. His droning guitar would heavily accent the simple lyrics of his hit songs such as "Boogie Chillen" and "Boom Boom" to make his blues sound like no other. Blues for Dummies *describes Hooker's playing:*

> Hooker is often called the "King of the Boogie" and his driving, rhythmic approach to guitar playing has become an integral element of the blues sound and style. [Hooker's 1948 debut hit "Boogie Chillen"] was considered something of an anachronism. Except for his thunderous electric guitar, Hooker's one-chord and two-chord modal stylings sounded very much like those of a Delta blues artist from the 1920s. But Hooker's music is altogether more fierce and rhythmic than old Delta blues. Early in his career, he played solo for the most part—his dark, hypnotic voice and relentless foot-stomping his only accompaniment.

Lonnie Brooks, Cub Koda, and Wayne Baker Brooks. *Blues for Dummies.* New York: IDG Books Worldwide, 1998, p. 116.

One way to determine the historical importance of a musician is to consider how many other musicians he or she has influenced. The list of legendary guitarists who owe a debt to King includes bluesmen Jimmy Page, Buddy Guy, Robert Cray, and Elmore James as well as rock star Jimi Hendrix.

The Blues Goes On and On

George "Buddy" Guy was one of the best blues guitarists that King inspired. Born in Lettsworth, Louisiana, on

July 30, 1936, Guy moved to Chicago in 1955, became a member of the Muddy Waters band, and in 1958 began making records. Listed thirtieth on *Rolling Stone*'s list of the 100 Greatest Guitarists, Guy has had a long career and was still performing in 2012. Guy is a dramatic showman who plays loudly and aggressively and influenced many other musicians including Eric Clapton, a contemporary rock and blues guitarist. Clapton once said, "Buddy is the last generation of the true blues musician as we know them. He knows the language and speaks it as I imagine he always did. He's the last, one-of-a-kind, he-man of the blues [and] guitar heroes."[127]

Clapton, who is ranked second on *Rolling Stone*'s list of guitarists, has written that Robert Johnson was his greatest musical inspiration. Thus the lineage of Clapton and many of today's other great blues and rock guitarists extends all the way back to the 1920s when "Blind" Lemon Jefferson and other blues singers began making records. Since then, a rural style of music once known only in the South has evolved into music that is modern and exciting enough to thrill the entire world.

CHAPTER 6

White Blues

O ne reason that the blues was unique when African Americans created it in the nineteenth century is that most of them had no formal training in music. Another reason is that segregation kept blacks and whites apart from each other socially, which meant blacks had little input from whites in conceiving the first truly original American music. In 1960 Willie B. Thomas, a guitar player from Scotlandville, Louisiana, explained those factors to Paul Oliver:

> It's not very much of song that Negro got from white, because Negro people always was a kind of singing people. You see, we was kind of a little different; we were a segregated bunch down among the white people. The white man could get education and he could learn proper things like read a note, and the Negro couldn't. All he had to get from his music was what God gave him in his heart. And that's the only thing he got. And he didn't get that from the white man. God give it to him.[128]

But when the blues began to emerge from the rural South, that black music began to influence white music. Music historian Earl L. Stewart says that popular and respected white composers began using the blues in their music:

> White composers like Irving Berlin, George Gershwin, and Jerome Kern were obviously aware of blues

elements and often incorporated them into their music. The craze for "blues" type songs in the 1920s and 1930s led many popular composers to [put] blue notes and other elements of the blues scale into their compositions.[129]

The most famous early piece the blues influenced was Gershwin's "Rhapsody in Blue," which premiered on February 12, 1924. Gershwin used blue notes in the long composition, which became an instant classic. Blues influences can also be heard in Gershwin's *Porgy and Bess*, which many music historians consider to be the twentieth century's most important American opera. *Porgy and Bess* is about poor blacks in Charleston, South Carolina, and includes classic songs such as "Summertime," "Bess, You Is My Woman Now," and "It Ain't Necessarily So." The opera was controversial when it debuted in 1935 because of its all-black cast.

The blues continued to influence American music in many ways, and white musicians and singers even began to sing and play the blues.

Early White Blues

In 1920 Mamie Smith became the first African American to record a blues song when she sang "Crazy Blues," but the first white singer to record a blues song was Sophie Tucker in 1917 when she sang "St. Louis Blues." (In fact, Tucker was originally supposed to record "Crazy Blues" for Okeh Records, and Smith filled in after Tucker fell ill.) Tucker was born Sonia Kalish in Tulchyn, Ukraine, on January 13, 1886, and her family immigrated to the United States when she was an infant. Tucker learned how to sing the blues by listening to black singers and asking them for advice. Classic blues star Alberta Hunter, however, refused Tucker's request: "Sophie Tucker sent her maid, Belle, for me to come to her dressing room and teach her songs, but I never would."[130] However, Tucker's piano player would listen to Hunter and tell her how to mimic Hunter's blues style.

Another white singer who recorded "St. Louis Blues" was Marion Harris. The popular American singer wanted to

Ragtime and jazz legend Sophie Tucker was the first performer to record a blues song in 1917. She is seen here in London, England, in 1928.

record the song so much that in 1920 she left Victor Records for Columbia Records because her old recording company would not let her do it. The fact that Harris was white did not bother W.C. Handy, who had written the song. In his autobiography, Handy praises Harris for her singing: "Miss Harris had used our [blues] numbers in her act for a long time, and she sang blues so well that people sometimes thought that the singer was colored."[131]

Many early country-and-western stars sang blues, including A.P. Carter, a member of the Carter Family Band in the 1920s. Carter learned the blues from his friend Lesley "Esley" Riddle, a black singer and guitar player. The Carter Family's biggest hit was "Worried Man Blues" in 1930. The song, about a man who is falsely imprisoned, includes the lyrics "It takes a worried man to sing a worried song, It takes a worried man to sing a worried song, I'm worried now but I won't be worried long."[132] The song's lyrics were in the traditional AAB blues pattern.

In the next several decades Barbara Dane, who was born in Arkansas on May 12, 1927, but grew up in Detroit,

Michigan, became one of the most prominent whites to sing the blues. Dane began singing and recording blues records in the 1950s and in 1959 became the first white singer profiled in *Ebony* magazine. In the magazine article, Dane explains that she was worried at first about singing the blues because she wanted to respect the black music: "I was very timid about approaching the blues. I had great respect for the material, and I'd be darned if I wanted to try to sing it without being able to do justice to it."[133] Dane sang the blues so well that she was still performing in 2012 at the age of eighty-five.

For several decades, however, the blues remained a predominantly black music in both its performers and the people who listened to it. That changed drastically after the advent of rock and roll.

The Blues Goes White

When rock and roll emerged as a powerful new musical genre in the 1950s, it had so many elements of blues and R&B that Arnold Shaw claims, "Rock n' roll was just a white imitation, a white adaptation of Negro [music]."[134] Rolling Stones guitarist and songwriter Keith Richards agrees with Shaw: "The music got called rock 'n' roll because it had gone white."[135] Prime evidence for their claim is Elvis Presley, the first rock superstar.

Presley was born on January 8, 1935, in Tupelo, Mississippi, and grew up loving the blues: "I dug the real low-down Mississippi singers, mostly [Lee Conley] 'Big Bill' Broonzy and [Arthur] 'Big Boy' Crudup, although they would scold me at home for listening to them."[136] The music his parents disliked was the same music that propelled Presley to stardom. The first song Presley recorded in October 1954 was "That's All Right (Mama)," which Crudup had released in 1946. His second was "Good Rockin' Tonight," which had been a hit in 1948 for Wynonie "Blues" Harris.

His versions of the songs were slightly different because Presley incorporated elements of southern and country-and-western music into them in a style that became known as rockabilly. But the blues was evident in Presley's style in the way he drew out and changed the pitch of notes when he

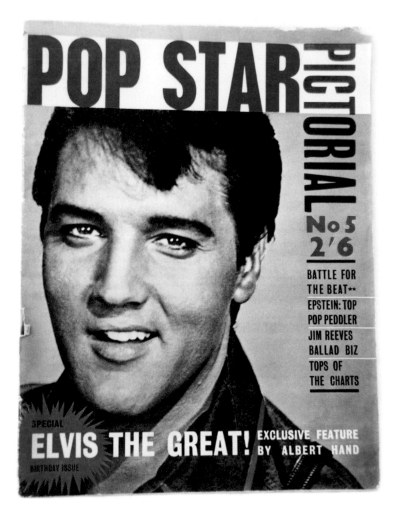

Elvis Presley, who incorporated blues and country elements into his music, was marketed as a rock and roll performer to appeal to white audiences.

sang, how he alternated rhythms, and in the deeply expressive way he sang the lyrics. Elijah Wald claims music companies classified Presley as a rock and roll singer because that was how they wanted to market him to whites:

After Presley's success, it became common for white southern singers who showed strong affinity for blues to be filed as rockers rather than country artists. There were some borderline figures. Johnny Cash recorded a few rockabilly discs but tended to be filed solidly on the country side of the divide, despite the deep blues sense that infused many of his best-known performances.[137]

Not many early American rock musicians or singers were as blues-oriented as Presley. Ironically, even though rock was a musical descendant of the blues, when it became popular in the 1950s and early 1960s it made the blues seem old fashioned to both whites and African Americans. B.B. King once admitted that, "For a large part of the sixties, I fell between the cracks of fashion [and] because I couldn't twist and shout, I was seen as a dinosaur."[138] Even worse, blues artists had trouble finding work performing and making records.

But in the early sixties, something strange happened—the British Invasion of bands such as the Beatles and the Rolling

The Paul Butterfield Blues Band

Paul Butterfield was born on December 17, 1942, in Chicago, Illinois, where as an adult he began visiting blues clubs and became devoted to the blues. In 1963 his Paul Butterfield Blues Band became one of the first integrated blues bands with bass guitarist Jerome Arnold and drummer Sam Lay, who had previously played with Howlin' Wolf's band. All Music Guide to the Blues *praises Butterfield as a pioneer of white blues:*

> Paul Butterfield was the first white harmonica player to develop a style original and powerful enough to place him in the pantheon of true blues greats. It's impossible to underestimate the importance of the doors Butterfield opened: before he came to prominence, white American musicians treated the blues with cautious respect, afraid of coming off as inauthentic. Not only did Butterfield clear the way for white musicians to build upon blues tradition (instead of merely replicating it), but his storming sound was a major catalyst to bringing electric Chicago blues to white audiences who'd previously considered acoustic Delta blues the only really genuine article.

All Music Guide to the Blues. Ann Arbor: All Media Guide, 2005, p. 91.

Stones resuscitated the blues. Unlike their American counterparts, British stars such as Paul McCartney and Mick Jagger revered older blues artists such as Muddy Waters and began to record their own versions of old blues classics.

The British Love the Blues

By the time the Beatles came to the United States for the first time on February 7, 1964, their records had already been smash hits in the United States for months. After landing in New York City, New York, the Beatles held a news conference. When reporters asked members of the band what they most wanted to see in the United States, they replied Muddy Waters and Elias "Bo Diddley" Bates. The Beatles were shocked when reporters did not recognize the names of the two blues greats and told them, "You Americans don't seem to know your most famous citizens."[139] Although the Beatles loved the blues, there were only traces of straight blues in their songs, such as John Lennon's harmonica playing in their 1962 hit "Love Me Do."

British rock stars had grown up listening to the blues because of Europe's fascination with that music. Starting with Lee Conley "Big Bill" Broonzy in 1949, blues stars such as Huddie "Lead Belly" Ledbetter, B.B. King, and Sister Rosetta Tharpe toured Europe and made the blues popular. Among the British rockers who loved the blues were Mick Jagger and Keith Richards of the Rolling Stones. The group even took its name from one of Muddy's songs—"Rollin' Stone"—and one of the band's greatest hits was "I Can't Get No Satisfaction," their version of a Muddy Waters song titled "I Can't Be Satisfied." In a foreword Richards wrote for a Muddy Waters biography, he explains that he first heard the blues great on a record Jagger had:

> [We] went 'round to his house, and he played me Muddy and I said, "Wow, *again*." And about ten hours later, I was still going, "Okay, *again*." When I heard "Still a Fool" and "Hoochie Coochie, Man"—that is the most powerful music I've ever heard. The most expressive.[140]

The blues influenced many other British bands and a few, such as John Mayall and the Bluesbreakers played nothing but blues. The fascination English rockers had for the blues and their devotion to blues greats revived interest in the blues in the United States. This was partly because British bands hired blues stars to open for them in sold-out performances across the nation. When King appeared with the Rolling Stones at the Fillmore West theater in San Francisco, California, he was overwhelmed by his reception from a mostly white audience: "By the time I strapped on Lucille [his guitar], every single person in the place was standing up and cheering like crazy. For the first time in my career, I got a standing ovation *before* I played. Couldn't help but cry."[141]

Even though more Americans began listening to black blues stars, there were also plenty of white blues stars to entertain them.

White Male Stars

Elvis Presley is considered the first king of rock and roll, but he also recorded blues songs such as "A Mess of Blues" and "Mean Woman Blues." Francis Davis claims, "He was one of the finest white blues singers."[142] Presley's 1955 version of "Mystery Train," a blues standard Herman "Junior" Parker recorded in 1953, is included on many collections of great blues songs. *Rolling Stone* magazine ranks it seventy-seventh on its list of the 500 Greatest Songs of All Time and claims it "is one of Presley's most haunting songs, a stark blues number [in which Presley] added a final verse—'Train . . . took my baby, but it never will again'—capped by a celebratory falsetto whoop that transformed a pastoral about death into a song about the power to overcome it."[143] The "train" in the melancholy song is a euphemism for death that took away the woman he loved.

Eric Clapton was born March 30, 1945, in England, and grew up wanting to become a painter. But at the age of fifteen Clapton suddenly decided to become a musician after listening to an album of Robert Johnson songs, including "Hellhound On My Trail." In his autobiography, Clapton writes that hearing Johnson's music for the first time was one of the most powerful experiences of his life:

B.B. King Praises White Blues Artists

Some African American blues artists, critics, and historians believe only blacks can perform authentic blues. Legendary blues great B.B. King is not one of them. In his autobiography, King writes:

> Because this country is so predominantly white, it's only logical that white boys have had the most impact in keeping twelve-bar blues alive. Englishman Eric Clapton is devoted to the blues and never stops paying tribute to his masters. For that, I pay tribute to him. Eric [plays] the blues as well as anyone and better than most. Bonnie Raitt is a white woman who has devoted her career to boosting black blues. She's a tireless fighter for blues pioneers and a great performer who happens to be the best slide guitarist out there, bar none. Of all the white guys, though, Stevie Ray Vaughan earned a place of his own. I loved him. [He] played with such incredible technique and genuine soul that he became the boldest guitarist of his generation.

B.B. King with David Ritz. *Blues All Around Me: The Autobiography of B.B. King.* New York: Avon, 1996, p. 294.

At first the music almost repelled me, it was so intense, and this man made no attempt to sugarcoat what he was trying to say or play. It was hard-core, more than anything I had ever heard. After a few listenings, I realized that on some level, I had found the master, and that following this man's example would be my life's work.[144]

In 1963 Clapton began playing with the Yardbirds, a rock band, but left two years later to join John Mayall's band and concentrate on the blues. Although Clapton is a fine blues singer, his guitar wizardry in both blues and rock and roll has always overshadowed his powerful vocals. Steven Van Zandt is a respected guitarist himself as a member of Bruce Springsteen's E Street Band. Van Zandt says Clapton's creativity in interpreting old blues guitar "licks"—creative bursts of music guitarists invent—changed guitar playing forever. He also says Clapton was always at his best playing blues:

Eric Clapton is the most important and influential guitar player that has ever lived, is still living or ever

Eric Clapton's exceptional guitar skills have made him very influential in both blues and rock and roll.

will live. [His song "Layla" is] Clapton's most original interpretation of the blues, because the hellhounds on his trail had a face: unrequited love.[145]

In 2004, Clapton paid tribute to Johnson by recording an album of his songs titled *Me and Mr. Johnson*. Despite being

Joe Bonamassa

In 2009 Joe Bonamassa was named Best Blues Guitarist in *Guitar Player* magazine's Readers' Choice Awards for the third consecutive year. Not bad for a twenty-two-year-old white guitarist born in New Hartford, New York. Bonamassa is perhaps the best of the younger, white blues artists like Kenny Wayne Shepherd and Jonny Lang. Bonamassa respects older blues greats like B.B. King and John Lee Hooker and has said he feels fortunate to have played with them. But in an interview in 2009, Bonamassa admitted that he was influenced more by white British blues musicians than African American stars of the past:

> I just thought the British blues was hipper [and] you'd see pictures of these young kids singing the blues and that really related to me. It had that swagger to it that I didn't really get initially when I listened to the originals, the American greats, who I subsequently understood. But I was listening to the English stuff and Irish guys like Gary Moore and Rory Gallagher way before I was into Muddy Waters and Robert Johnson and that kind of stuff.

Joe Bonamassa performs in Hungary in 2009. This guitar virtuoso is a contemporary blues star for a new generation.

Trevor Hodgett. "Joe Bonamassa Interview." *Blues in Britain*, November 2008. www.bluesinbritain.org/joe-bonamassa-interview.

a guitar virtuoso, Clapton admits it was difficult to duplicate Johnson's solo acoustic guitar playing because it was so complicated: "I've always found it necessary to delegate parts of his arrangements to other musicians."[146] Clapton by then had been duplicating his hero's style for nearly five decades—his first lead vocal on a record in 1966 was a cover of Johnson's "Ramblin' On My Mind."

The history of the blues has been dominated by guitar players. One of the most influential modern blues guitarists was Stephen "Stevie Ray" Vaughan. Born on October 3, 1954, in Dallas, Texas, Vaughan died in a helicopter crash on August 27, 1990, in East Troy, Wisconsin, after a performance with several blues greats including Clapton and George "Buddy" Guy. Vaughan began playing guitar at age seven while listening to records of Muddy Waters, Buddy Guy, B.B. King, and Albert King; by high school he was performing in local clubs. His recording career began in 1970 and he had many hits with his band Double Trouble, including "Pride and Joy" and "The Sky Is Crying."

Vaughan was a brilliant guitarist and an emotional singer. But Tom Piazza believes his greatest contribution to the blues was to help make them popular again after a period in the 1970s and 1980s when many people had lost interest. Piazza writes:

> [Vaughan] captured the ears of young Americans with a driving rock sound infused with the blues. His guitar style was more fierce than nuanced [as in the blues], but his flamboyance and monochromatic spitfire-like attack excited diverse audiences. "Pride and Joy," a tight, hard driving shuffle representative of his up-tempo work, is Vaughan's signature tune.[147]

There are a host of white male blues stars. The list of white female blues stars is shorter but includes one who could sing the blues with as much emotion and conviction as any black woman: Janis Joplin.

Female Blues Stars

In *Blues for Dummies*, co-authors Lonnie Brooks, Cub Koda, and Wayne Baker Brooks state unequivocally that, "Janis was, quite simply, the greatest white female blues singer of her time or any time."[148] Joplin was born on January 19, 1943, in Port Arthur, Texas. In high school, she listened to blues records, including those of classic blues singer Bessie Smith, who became her vocal role model. Joplin once said:

> I listened to them and I liked them a lot better than what I heard on the radio. They seemed to have some sincerity to them. I just really fell in love with [Bessie]. For the first few years I sang, I sang just like Bessie Smith. I copied her a lot, sang all her songs.[149]

Joplin moved to San Francisco in the early 1960s and began singing the blues. She became the lead vocalist for several groups including the Kozmic Blues Band. One of Joplin's biggest hits was her 1967 version of "Ball and Chain," a song previously recorded by Willie Mae "Big Mama" Thornton that compares being in love to wearing a metal ball and chain. Joplin's expressive voice—she alternately sings the lyrics in both a soft, pain-filled voice and shouting, wailing, and moaning—convinced everyone that loving someone could be painful emotionally.

B.B. King once said, "Janis Joplin sings the blues as hard as any black person."[150] Joplin also lived hard, dying of a heroin overdose on October 4, 1970, in Los Angeles, California, at age twenty-seven. Joplin had only a few major hits but remains a blues and rock icon today because of her powerful singing and personality. Singer Rosanne Cash, a daughter of country music legend Johnny Cash, once said of Joplin:

> The beauty and the power of Janis Joplin as a singer is her complete lack of fear. She held nothing back. She went to the edge every time she opened her mouth. She sang from her toes and from her soul. She could also destroy you when she got vulnerable, like on "Me and Bobby McGee," where you saw the little girl underneath. [She] was a very fierce, very beautiful bright light that burned out way, way too quickly.[151]

Another legendary white blues artist is Bonnie Raitt. The daughter of Broadway musical star John Raitt, she was born November 8, 1949, in Burbank, California, and began playing guitar as a youngster. She attended Radcliffe College in Cambridge, Massachusetts, with the intent of going to

Janis Joplin is considered one of the best white female blues singers of all time.

Africa to help people there have a better life. Instead, she fell in love with the blues and began a musical career before graduating. Like Joplin, Raitt was influenced by a classic blues singer—Sippie Wallace—but Raitt's singing style is smoother and more sophisticated. One of her most moving songs is "I'm in the Mood." Raitt won her first Grammy Award in 1990 for that duet with blues great John Lee Hooker for Best Traditional Blues Recording. Raitt is also celebrated for her guitar playing. *Rolling Stone* magazine ranks her eighty-ninth on its list of 100 Greatest Guitarists:

> Starting with her acoustic slide workout on 1971's "Walking Blues," Raitt rolled out a fearsome repertoire of blues licks, fingerpicking with the best and wielding a slide like an old master. Most of all, she set a crucial precedent: When guitar was still considered a man's game by many, Raitt busted down that barrier through sheer verve and skill.[152]

One female blues guitarist who followed Raitt's path is Susan Tedeschi. Born on November 9, 1970, in Boston, Massachusetts, she fell in love with the blues by listening to her dad's records of singers such as Mississippi John Hurt. In 1994 Tedeschi started her own band and three years later began recording songs. Tedeschi, who is married to blues guitarist Derek Trucks, was influenced by both Joplin and Raitt, and her singing style is a mix of the two. Tedeschi explains what drew her to the blues:

> The music is so universal. It talks about the relationship between a man and a woman. That's what Son House used to say: "Blues is about a man and a woman—everything else is monkey junk." He's got a point. You're talking about everyday-life stuff that people can relate to because it's funny or it's raunchy or it's sad or it's uplifting and exciting. It makes sense that all kinds of people are into it.[153]

The universal appeal of the blues has kept it popular into the twenty-first century, and that aspect of the blues will continue to allow this original American music to influence generations of musicians for years to come.

Introduction: The Heart of the Blues

1. Quoted in Nancy Benac. "Obama Sings 'Sweet Home Chicago' During Blues Concert At White House." *Huffington Post*, February 21, 2012. www.huffingtonpost.com/2012/02/21/obama-sings-sweet-home-chicago_n_1292576.html.

2. Barack Obama. "President Barack Obama Delivers Remarks at a Performance at the White House Event Celebrating Blues Music in Recognition of Black History Month." Federal Document Clearing House Political Transcript, February 21, 2012.

3. Quoted in Elijah Wald. *The Blues: A Very Short Introduction*. New York: Oxford University Press, 2010, p. 111.

4. Quoted in Paul Oliver. *The Story of The Blues*. Lebanon, NH: Northeastern University Press, 1997, p. 3.

5. Quoted in Buzzy Jackson. *A Bad Woman Feeling Good: Blues and the Women Who Sing Them*. New York: W. W. Norton, 2005, p. 11.

6. Quoted in Alan Lomax. *The Land Where the Blues Began*. New York: Pantheon, 1993, p. 466.

7. Quoted in Lomax. *The Land Where the Blues Began*, p. 566.

8. Quoted in Paul Oliver. *Blues Fell This Morning: Meaning in the Blues*. New York: Cambridge University Press, 1960, p. 113.

9. Quoted in Peter Keepnews. "Etta James Dies at 73; Voice Behind 'At Last.'" *New York Times*, January 20, 2012. www.nytimes.com/2012/01/21/arts/music/etta-james-singer-dies-at-73.html?_r=2.

Chapter 1: An African American Music

10. Quoted in Burton W. Peretti. *Lift Every Voice: The History of African American Music*. New York: Rowman and Littlefield, 2009, p. 186.

11. John W. Work. *American Negro Songs and Spirituals*. New York: Bonanza, 1940, p. 1.

12. Quoted in James Haskins. *Black Music in America: A History Through Its People*. New York: HarperCollins, 1987, p. 3.

13. Eileen Southern. *The Music of Black Americans: A History*. New York: W. W. Norton, 1997, p. 21.

14. Quoted in Paul Oliver et al. *Yonder Come the Blues: The Evolution of a*

Genre. New York: Cambridge University Press, 2001, p. 12.

15. Quoted in Giles Oakley. *The Devil's Music: A History of the Blues*. New York: Taplinger, 1977, pp. 11–12.

16. Quoted in *American Roots Music: Instruments and Innovation*. Public Broadcasting System. www.pbs.org/americanrootsmusic/pbs_arm_ii_banjo.html.

17. Southern. *The Music of Black Americans*, p. 195.

18. Southern. *The Music of Black Americans*, p. 26.

19. Oliver et al. *Yonder Come the Blues*, p. 35.

20. Quoted in Earl L. Stewart. *Black Music: An Introduction*. New York: Schirmer, 1998, p. 44.

21. Quoted in Samuel Charters. *The Bluesmen*. New York: Oak Publications, 1967, p. 7.

22. LeRoi Jones (Amiri Baraka). *Blues People: Negro Music in White America*. New York: Quill, 1999, p. 42.

23. "Swing Low Sweet Chariot." Negro Spirituals.com. www.negrospirituals.com/news-song/swing_low_sweet_chariot_swing_lo.htm.

24. Southern. *The Music of Black Americans*, p. 334.

25. Peretti. *Lift Every Voice*, p. 24.

26. "Lay This Body Down." Folk Songs from Digital Tradition. www.8notes.com/digital_tradition/LAYBODY.asp.

27. Quoted in Oakley. *The Devil's Music*, p. 31.

28. Quoted in Peter Hanley. "Portraits from Jelly Roll's New Orleans."

2002. www.doctorjazz.co.uk/portnewor.html.

29. Work. *American Negro Songs and Spirituals*, p. 32.

30. W.C. Handy. *Father of the Blues: An Autobiography of W.C. Handy*. New York: Macmillan, 1941, p. 74.

31. Southern. *The Music of Black Americans*, p. 334.

Chapter 2: The Blues Evolve

32. Paul Oliver. *Broadcasting the Blues: Black Blues in the Segregation Era*. New York: Routledge, 2006, p. 3.

33. Paul Garon. *Blues and the Poetic Spirit*. New York: De Capo, 1978, p. 33.

34. Dick Weissman. *Blues: The Basics*. New York: Routledge, 2005, p. 23.

35. W.C. Handy. "St. Louis Blues." www.lyrics.com/st-louis-blues-lyrics-wc-handy.html.

36. "Blind" Lemon Jefferson. "Rising High Water Blues." www.harptab.com/lyrics/ly2716.shtml.

37. Quoted in Noah Adams. "Singing the Blues about 1927's Delta Floods." *Day to Day*, National Public Radio, September 23, 2005. www.pr.org/templates/transcript/transcript.php?storyId=4860785.

38. Southern. *The Music of Black Americans*, p. 336.

39. Quoted in Francis Davis. *The History of the Blues*. New York: Hyperion, 1995, pp. 59–60.

40. Work. *American Negro Songs and Spirituals*, p. 29.

41. Arnold Shaw. *Honkers and Shout-*

ers: *The Golden Years of Rhythm and Blues*. New York: Macmillan, 1978, p. 4.

42. Daphne Duval Harrison. *Black Pearls: Blues Queens of the 1920s*. New Brunswick, CT: Rutgers University Press, 1988, p 11.

43. Angela Y. Davis. *Blues Legacies and Black Feminism: Gertrude "Ma" Rainey, Bessie Smith, and Billie Holliday*. New York: Pantheon, 1998, p. xiii.

44. "Blind" Lemon Jefferson. "Got The Blues." www.blueslyrics.com.ar/Blind-Lemon-Jefferson/GotThe Blues.html.

45. Oliver. *Broadcasting the Blues*, p. 58.

46. Oliver. *The Story of the Blues*, p. 41.

47. Robert Palmer. *Deep Blues: A Musical and Cultural History of the Mississippi Delta*. New York: Penguin, 1981, p. 107.

48. Wald. *The Blues*, p. 14.

49. Weissman. *Blues*, pp. 85–86.

50. Davis. *The History of the Blues*, p. 176.

51. Muddy Waters. "Country Blues Lyrics." www.lyricsfreak.com/m/muddy+waters/country+blues _20173801.html.

52. Lomax. *The Land Where the Blues Began*, p. xi.

Chapter 3: Fruits of the Blues

53. Tom Piazza. *The Blues: A Musical Journey*. Santa Monica, CA: Hip-O Records, 2003, pp. 41–42.

54. Quoted in "Martin Scorsese Presents the Blues." September 2003. www.pbs.org/theblues.

55. Southern. *The Music of Black Americans*, p. 368.

56. Shaw. *Honkers and Shouters*, p. 13.

57. Quoted in William Ferris. *Give My Poor Heart Ease: Voice of the Mississippi Blues*. Chapel Hill: University of North Carolina Press, 2009, p. 11.

58. Thomas A. Dorsey. "Precious Lord Take My Hand." www.kentangen .com/sing/Lyrics/Precious%20 Lord%20lyrics.htm.

59. Quoted in Lindsay Terry. "The Story Behind the Song 'Peace in the Valley.'" The Christian Broadcasting Network. www.cbn.com /spirituallife/devotions/terry _peace.aspx.

60. Quoted in Donald E. Wilcock with Buddy Guy. *Damn Right I've Got the Blues: Buddy Guy and the Blues Roots of Rock-and-Roll*. San Francisco: Woodford, 1993, p. 39.

61. Shaw. *Honkers and Shouters*, p. xvi.

62. Southern. *The Music of Black Americans*, p. 514.

63. Louis Jordan. "Hard Lovin' Blues." www.louisjordan.com/lyrics/Hard LovinBlues.aspx?l=1.

64. Quoted in Peter Guralnick, Robert Santelli, Holly George-Warren, and Christopher John Farley, eds. *Martin Scorsese Presents the Blues: A Musical Journey*. New York: Amistad, 2003, p. 36.

65. Shaw. *Honkers and Shouters*, p. 64.

66. Oliver. *The Story of the Blues*, p. 189.

67. Stewart. *Black Music*, p. 223.
68. Quoted in Ray Charles. "I Got A Woman." www.lyricsdepot.com/ray-charles/i-got-a-woman.html.
69. Quoted in Jimmie Rodgers. "Blue Yodel No.1 Tabs." www.allcountrytabs.com/tabs/jimmie-rodgers/blue-yodel-no1-10818.html.
70. Quoted in Oliver et al. *Yonder Come the Blues*, p. 191.
71. Quoted in Guralnick, Santelli, George-Warren, and Farley, eds. *Martin Scorsese Presents the Blues*, p. 173.
72. Quoted in Shaw. *Honkers and Shouters*, p. 64.
73. Quoted in Guralnick, Santelli, George-Warren, and Farley, eds. *Martin Scorsese Presents the Blues*, p. 57.
74. Quoted in Guralnick, Santelli, George-Warren, and Farley, eds. *Martin Scorsese Presents the Blues*, p. 187.

Chapter 4: Famous Blues Women

75. Quoted in Mamie Smith and Her Jazz Hounds. "Crazy Blues Lyrics (1920)." www.justsomelyrics.com/1760883/Mamie-Smith-%26-Her-Jazz-Hounds-Crazy-Blues-(1920)-Lyrics.
76. Quoted in Oliver. *Broadcasting the Blues*, p. 132.
77. Davis. *Blues Legacies and Black Feminism*, p. 138.
78 Harrison. *Black Pearls*, p. 70.
79. Quoted in Davis. *Blues Legacies and Black Feminism*, p. 29.
80. Davis. *The History of the Blues*, p. 86.
81. Oliver. *The Story of the Blues*, p. 68.
82. Southern. *The Music of Black Americans*, p. 373.
83. Piazza. *The Blues*, pp. 41–42.
84. Bessie Smith. "Nobody Knows You When You're Down And Out." www.lyricstime.com/bessie-smith-nobody-knows-you-when-you%27re-down-and-out-lyrics.html.
85. Quoted in Lonnie Brooks, Cub Koda, and Wayne Baker Brooks. *Blues for Dummies*. New York: IDG Books Worldwide, 1998, p. 48.
86. Oliver. *The Story of the Blues*, p. 122.
87. Quoted in Wald. *The Blues*, p. 48.
88. Quoted in Jackson. *A Bad Woman Feeling Good*, p. 98.
89. Quoted in Geoffrey C. Ward. "Billie Holiday." *American Heritage*, December 1994, p. 14.
90. Angela Davis. "Back to the Roots." *Time*, June 8, 1998, p. 169.
91. Quoted in Michael Ross. "Forgotten Heroes: Sister Rosetta Tharpe." *Premier Guitar*, May 2011. www.premierguitar.com/Magazine/Issue/2011/May/Forgotten_Heroes_Sister_Rosetta_Tharpe.aspx.
92. Quoted in Ross. "Forgotten Heroes."
93. Quoted in Sister Rosetta Tharpe. *Gospel 'N' Soul Revival*. The Great American Music Company, 2009.
94. Quoted in Gayle F. Wald. *Shout Sister, Shout: The Untold Story of Rock-and-Roll Trailblazer Sister*

Rosetta Tharpe. Boston: Beacon, 2007, p. 184.

95. Quoted in Wald. *Shout Sister, Shout*, p. 70.

96. Quoted in David Ritz. "The Immortal Hits, Wild Life and Tragic Death of One of Blues, Rock and R&B's All-Time Greats." *Rolling Stone*, February 16, 2012, p. 26.

97. Quoted in Ritz. "The Immortal Hits, Wild Life and Tragic Death of One of Blues, Rock and R&B's All-Time Greats," p. 26.

98. Quoted in Etta James. "At Last." www.azlyrics.com/lyrics/etta james/atlast.html.

99. Quoted in Ritz. "The Immortal Hits, Wild Life and Tragic Death of One of Blues, Rock and R&B's All-Time Greats," p. 26.

100. Quoted in Keepnews. "Etta James Dies at 73; Voice Behind 'At Last.'"

101. Quoted in David Prince. "Koko Taylor Talks About Her Life in the Blues." *Santa Fe New Mexican*, May 13, 1994, p. 33.

102. Ben Ratliff. "Koko Taylor." *Rolling Stone*, May 28, 1998, p. 4.

103. Quoted in Renée Montagne. "Blues Queen Koko Taylor Dies at 80." *Morning Edition*, National Public Radio, June 4, 2009.

104. Quoted in Prince. "Koko Taylor Talks About Her Life in the Blues," p. 33.

105. Quoted in Memphis Minnie McCoy. www.findagrave.com/cgi-bin/fg.cgi?page=gr&GRid=14639079.

Chapter 5: Famous Blues Men

106. Piazza. *The Blues*, pp. 41–42.

107. Quoted in Davis. *The History of the Blues*, p. 63.

108. Oliver. *Broadcasting the Blues*, p. 23.

109. Piazza. *The Blues*, pp. 41–42.

110. Charley Patton. "High Sherriff Blues." www.lyricstime.com/charley-patton-high-sheriff-blues-lyrics.html.

111. Oliver. *Broadcasting the Blues*, p. 23.

112. Quoted in Samuel Charters. "Seeking the Greatest Bluesman." *American Heritage*, July–August 1991, p. 50.

113. Oakley. *The Devil's Music*, p. 219.

114. Quoted in liner notes for *Big Bill Broonzy Amsterdam Live Concerts 1953*. Belgium: Munich Records, 2006.

115. Quoted in Shaw. *Honkers and Shouters*, p. 24.

116. Big Bill Broonzy. "Black, Brown and White." www.lyricstime.com/big-bill-broonzy-just-a-dream-lyrics.html.

117. Tony Russell. *The Blues: From Robert Johnson to Robert Cray*. New York: Schirmer, 1997, p. 50.

118. Quoted in Robert Gordon. *Can't Be Satisfied: The Life and Times of Muddy Waters*. New York: Little, Brown and Company, 2002, p. xv.

119. Quoted in Gordon. *Can't Be Satisfied*, p. 79.

120. Quoted in Gordon. *Can't Be Satisfied*, p. 490.

121. Quoted in Palmer. *Deep Blues*, p. 255.

122. Quoted in Shaw. *Honkers and Shouters*, p. 114.

123. B.B. King with David Ritz. *Blues All Around Me: The Autobiography of B.B. King*. New York: Avon, 1996, p. 41.

124. B.B. King. "The Thrill Is Gone." www.stlyrics.com/lyrics/martin scorsesebestoftheblues/thethrillis gone.htm.

125. Quoted in Billy Gibbons. "100 Greatest Guitarists, No. 6, B.B. King." *Rolling Stone*. www.rolling stone.com/music/lists/100 -greatest-guitarists-20111123/b-b -king-19691231.

126. King with Ritz. *Blues All Around Me*, p. 127.

127. Quoted in Wilcock with Guy. *Damn Right I've Got the Blues*, p. 93.

Chapter 6: White Blues

128. Quoted in Oliver et al. *Yonder Come the Blues*, p. 49.

129. Stewart. *Black Music*, p. 59.

130. Quoted in Jackson. *A Bad Woman Feeling Good*, p. 25.

131. Quoted in Marion Harris. www .redhotjazz.com/marionharris. html.

132. Quoted in "The Carter Family, Will The Circle Be Unbroken." The Carter Songbook, *American Experience*, Public Broadcasting System, 2003. www.pbs.org/wgbh /amex/carterfamily/sfeature/sf _song_pop_03_qry.html.

133. Quoted in "White Blues Singer, Blonde Keeps Blues Alive." *Ebony*, November 1959, p. 154.

134. Shaw. *Honkers and Shouters*, p. 73.

135. Quoted in Mick Jagger, Keith Richards, Charlie Watts, and Ronnie Wood. *According to The Rolling Stones*. San Francisco: Chronicle, 2003, p. 15.

136. Shaw. *Honkers and Shouters*, p. xxiii.

137. Wald. *The Blues*, p. 108.

138. King with Ritz. *Blues All Around Me*, p. 212.

139. Quoted in Lomax. *The Land Where the Blues Began*, p. 406.

140. Gordon. *Can't Be Satisfied*, p. xi.

141. King with Ritz. *Blues All Around Me*, p. 240.

142. Davis. *The History of the Blues*, p. 210.

143. "500 Greatest Songs of All Time, No. 77, Elvis Presley, 'Mystery Train.'" *Rolling Stone*. www.roll ingstone.com/music/lists/the -500-greatest-songs-of-all-time -20110407/elvis-presley-mystery -train-19691231.

144. Quoted in Sheila Byrd. "100 Years After Bluesman Robert Johnson's Birth, Legacy Sparks Tributes." Provincecity.com, May 5, 2011. www.provincecity.com/MS /Hazlehurst/news/100_years_after _bluesman_robert-4759397/.

145. Steven "Little Steven" Van Zandt. "100 Greatest Artists of All Time, No. 55, Eric Clapton." www.rolling stone.com/music/lists/100-greatest -artists-of-all-time-19691231/eric -clapton-19691231.

146. Quoted in Jenny Eliscu. "Eric Clapton." *Rolling Stone*, March, 4, 2004, p. 58.

147. Piazza. *The Blues*, p. 47.

148. Brooks, Koda, and Brooks. *Blues for Dummies*, p. 130.

149. Quoted in Jackson. *A Bad Woman Feeling Good*, p. 207.

150. Quoted in David Dalton. *Piece of My Heart: A Portrait of Janis Joplin.* New York: Da Capo, 1991, p. 38.

151. Quoted in Rosanne Cash. "Janis Joplin." *Rolling Stone*, April 14, 2004, p. 136.

152. Quoted in "100 Greatest Guitarists, No. 89, Bonnie Raitt." *Rolling Stone*, November 23, 2011. www.rollingstone.com/music/lists/100-greatest-guitarists-20111123/bonnie-raitt-19691231.

153. Quoted in David Hajdu. "Who's Got the Blues?" *Mother Jones*, September–October 2003, p. 76.

"Big Bill" Broonzy

Trouble in Mind, 2000

This collection showcases the work of Broonzy, who helped modernize the blues in the 1930s and 1940s with songs such as "Black, Brown and White" and "Mule Ridin' Blues."

Eric Clapton

From the Cradle, 1994

Clapton performs sixteen songs that highlight the England native's mastery of the blues.

Me and Mr. Johnson, 2004

Clapton performs fourteen songs by Robert Johnson, the blues legend who inspired him to become a musician.

Billie Holiday

Lady Day: The Best of Billie Holiday, 2001

On this album, one of the twentieth century's finest female singers shows her versatility in a variety of styles including the blues in songs such as "Billie's Blues."

John Lee Hooker

John Lee Hooker: The Definitive Collection, 2006

Hooker's interesting voice and percussive blues guitar style made him a star for decades. This album features hits such as "Boogie Chillen" and "Boom Boom."

Howlin' Wolf

Howlin' Wolf: His Best, 1997

On twenty songs including the blues standard "Killing Floor," Chester Arthur Burnett moans and growls songs while playing a mean electric guitar in the style that made him a blues legend.

Etta James

Etta James: Her Best, 1997

This twenty-song collection includes James's greatest hits, from the romantic ballad "At Last" to the sexy "Tell Mama."

"Blind" Lemon Jefferson

The Best of Blind Lemon Jefferson, 2000

This compilation displays the raw vocals and intricate acoustic guitar playing of the country blues singer from Texas on hit songs such as "Matchbox Blues."

Robert Johnson

Robert Johnson: The Complete Recordings, 1990

The forty-one tracks in this two-disc set are the entire recorded output of the most legendary and influential country blues singer.

Janis Joplin

Janis Joplin's Greatest Hits, 1999

This collection by the woman regarded as the greatest white female blues singer of all time includes her raw, powerful version of the blues classic "Ball and Chain."

B.B. King

B.B. King: The Ultimate Collection, 2005

This album has twenty-one hit songs by one of the greatest blues guitarists of all time, including "Three O'Clock Blues," the 1952 song that made him a star.

Huddie "Lead Belly" Ledbetter

Huddie Ledbetter's Best, 2002

This compilation displays Lead Belly's powerful, moaning voice and fine acoustic guitar playing on songs such as "Goodnight, Irene" and "Backwater Blues" that made him an early twentieth-century blues star.

Mississippi Fred McDowell

I Do Not Play No Rock 'N' Roll, 2006

This two-disc set shows why McDowell's smooth voice and creative electric guitar work on songs such as "61 Highway" and "Kokomo Me Baby" made him a national star during the 1960s blues resurgence.

Memphis Minnie

Memphis Minnie: Queen of Country Blues, 2003

Her acoustic guitar skill and amusing yet sexy voice earned Lizzie Douglas the title "Queen of Country Blues." This five-disc set includes some of her greatest hits, such as "Me and My Chauffeur Blues" and "Bumble Bee."

Charley Patton

Charley Patton: Founder of the Delta Blues, 1995

This collection showcases the work of the artist who made Delta blues popular with songs such as "High Water Everywhere," about the 1927 flood that devastated the South.

Bonnie Raitt

The Best of Bonnie Raitt, 2003

On this compilation, Raitt displays the fine electric guitar playing and passionate singing that made her a star on songs such as "Thing Called Love" and "Silver Lining."

Bessie Smith

Essential Bessie Smith, 1997

This two-disc set includes "Backwater Blues," "Need a Little Sugar in My Bowl," and other songs by the classic blues star dubbed "Empress of the Blues."

Koko Taylor

What It Takes: The Chess Years (Expanded Edition), 2009

On this compilation, Taylor shows why she was one of the greatest female blues singers of all time, with songs ranging from the raucous party song "Wang Dang Doodle" to the mournful "Blue Prelude."

Sister Rosetta Tharpe

The Gospel of the Blues, 2003

Best known as a gospel singer, Tharpe's powerful voice and electric guitar playing produced blues hits such as "Rock Me" and "I Want a Tall Skinny Papa."

Stevie Ray Vaughan

The Essential Stevie Ray Vaughan and Double Trouble, 2002

This two-disc set includes "Pride and Joy" and "The Sky Is Crying," two blues tunes that define the music of one of the greatest electric blues and rock guitarists.

Muddy Waters

Muddy Waters: The Definitive Collection, 2006

McKinley "Muddy Waters" Morganfield helped invent electric blues and influenced English rockers including the Rolling Stones. This collection features hits such as "I Can't Be Satisfied" and "Rollin' Stone."

Various Artists

The Blues: A Smithsonian Collection of Classic Blues Singers, 1993

This four-disc set is a vocal history of the blues and includes a well-written account of the music genre.

House of Blues: Essential Blues, 1995

The thirty-two songs in this collection include historic blues tunes recorded during the twentieth century by male and female singers.

House of Blues: Essential Women in Blues, 1997

The thirty songs in this collection include historic women blues singers such as Mamie Smith, Memphis Minnie, and Koko Taylor.

Martin Scorsese Presents the Blues—A Musical Journey, 2003

This five-disc compilation includes blues greats from every era singing historic blues songs.

Ultimate Blues Album, 2003

This two-disc set has thirty-six songs by most of the great modern blues singers and musicians.

AAB: The traditional blues lyrics format in which the first two lines of a song are nearly identical; the third line complements the thought of the first two and usually rhymes with them.

blue note: A note that is sung or played at a slightly lower pitch than the European major musical scale.

bottleneck guitar: Also called slide guitar; a style of guitar playing in which musicians place something on their finger—traditionally the rounded neck of a glass bottle—and slide it along guitar strings and depress them to vary the vibrating length and pitch of notes they play.

call and response: An African singing technique involving one singer and a second singer or group in which the first singer gives the "call" and the second singer or group gives a "response."

classic blues: The blues songs women sang in the 1920s to the accompaniment of jazz-style music.

country blues: Also called folk blues; traditional twelve-bar songs with an AAB lyric pattern that are performed by one person, usually a man playing an acoustic guitar.

Delta blues: A style of country blues that originated in southern Mississippi and that features strong rhythms and use of a bottleneck to play slide guitar.

electric blues: Also called Chicago blues or modern blues; music that evolved in Chicago, Illinois, in the 1940s and featured several musicians playing amplified instruments such as electric guitars and harmonicas.

field hollers: Songs that slaves and African American laborers sang while working; they are considered an early but crude form of the blues and other African American music.

Great Migration: The movement out of the South in the first half of the twentieth century by several million African Americans who desired to escape racism and have better lives.

griot: A West African term for someone who sang songs to recount oral traditions and histories.

jug band: Bands that used homemade and common instruments such as the kazoo, washtub, jug, and whiskey bottle as well as banjo, harmonica, or guitar.

juke joint: An African American establishment in the South that served alcohol and had musical entertainment.

jump blues: A style of blues played by

big bands in the 1930s and 1940s that combined elements of blues, jazz, and popular music.

melisma: An African singing technique, prevalent in modern music, in which a singer moves between several notes while singing a single syllable.

polyrhythm: A method of using two or more different rhythms in a song at the same time.

race records: The term for records made by African American artists from the early 1920s until 1949, when the category was changed to rhythm and blues.

rhythm and blues: A style of music that originated in the 1940s and was played by small bands with four or five musicians; it fused elements of the blues, gospel, and pop music.

rock and roll: A style of music that originated in the early 1950s; it combined elements of blues and country-and-western music, but its closest musical cousin was rhythm and blues.

shuffle: A style of music in which some notes with equal written time values are performed with unequal durations, usually as alternating long and short, to create unusual rhythms.

syncopation: The placement of rhythmic stresses, or accents, where they would not normally occur, or using a variety of rhythms to interrupt the overall regular rhythm in a musical composition.

twelve-bar blues: The standard format for country blues of twelve bars of music.

urban blues: A more sophisticated style of blues that developed in the 1930s and early 1940s and portrayed African American city life.

Books

Lonnie Brooks, Cub Koda, and Wayne Baker Brooks. *Blues for Dummies*. New York; IDG Books Worldwide, 1998. The authors of this book, all blues performers, discuss facets and personalities of the blues.

Samuel Charters. *The Bluesmen*. New York: Oak Publications, 1967. This book provides intriguing personal portraits of blues greats.

Robert Gordon. *Can't Be Satisfied: The Life and Times of Muddy Waters*. New York: Little, Brown and Company, 2002. This book details the biography of one of the most influential bluesmen.

Peter Guralnick, Robert Santelli, Holly George-Warren, and Christopher John Farley, eds. *Martin Scorsese Presents the Blues: A Musical Journey*. New York: Amistad, 2003. This companion book to the PBS documentary of the same name has historic photos and interesting articles about blues greats and the music genre's history.

Daphne Duval Harrison. *Black Pearls: Blues Queens of the 1920s*. New Brunswick, CT: Rutgers University Press, 1988. This book offers a history of the classic blues and the female stars that made it an important blues era.

James Haskins. *Black Music in America: A History Through Its People*. New York: HarperCollins, 1987. This book covers the history of African American music.

LeRoi Jones (Amiri Baraka). *Blues People: Negro Music in White America*. New York: Quill, 1999. This book ties the development of black music to sociological changes in the status of African Americans throughout U.S. history.

B.B. King with David Ritz. *Blues All Around Me: The Autobiography of B.B. King*. New York: Avon, 1996. The blues legend writes about his life, the blues, and racism he faced while growing up in Mississippi.

Alan Lomax. *The Land Where the Blues Began*. New York: Pantheon, 1993. Lomax covers his unique experiences in recording historic blues tunes, including his discovery of McKinley "Muddy Waters" Morganfield.

Giles Oakley. *The Devil's Music: A History of the Blues*. New York: Taplinger, 1977. This book provides an entertaining look at how the blues developed.

Paul Oliver. *The Story of the Blues*. Lebanon, NH: Northeastern University Press, 1997. The author of several books on the blues provides a comprehensive history of the development of the music genre.

Robert Palmer. *Deep Blues: A Musical and Cultural History of the Mississippi Delta*. New York: Penguin, 1981. A music critic covers the history of the blues.

Tony Russell. *The Blues: From Robert Johnson to Robert Cray*. New York, Schirmer, 1997. The author of this book profiles blues greats from different eras.

Arnold Shaw. *Honkers and Shouters: The Golden Years of Rhythm and Blues*. New York: Macmillan, 1978. This book offers a vibrant study of blues history focusing on the development of rhythm and blues.

Eileen Southern. *The Music of Black Americans: A History*. New York: W.W. Norton, 1997. This is one of the best books written on the historic development of black music.

Elijah Wald. *The Blues: A Very Short Introduction*. New York: Oxford University Press, 2010. This book provides a concise history of all eras of the blues.

Dick Weissman. *Blues: The Basics*. New York: Routledge, 2005. This book covers the musical structure of the blues.

Places to Visit

The Delta Blues Museum (www.deltabluesmuseum.org). This museum has displays on blues history and artifacts, including a small cabin that was the childhood home of McKinley "Muddy Waters" Morganfield. It is located in Clarksdale, Mississippi.

Websites

All Music: Blues (www.allmusic.com/genre/blues-ma0000002467). This website offers definitions of various blues styles as well as sample tracks and profiles of prominent blues musicians.

Blues Nexus (www.bluesnexus.com). This website has a history of the blues, biographies of blues greats, and other information on the blues.

Bluescentric(www.bluescentric.com). This website provides a history of the blues, biographies of blues greats, pictures, and other features.

Martin Scorsese Presents the Blues (www.pbs.org/theblues/index.html). Famed movie director Scorsese guided six other directors, including Clint Eastwood, in making short films that explore the history and personalities of the blues for a PBS series. This website features interviews and film clips from the series.

A Short Blues History (www.history-of-rock.com/blues.htm). This website features a brief history of the blues and its link to rock and roll.

INDEX

A

AAB lyric pattern, 31, 44, 53–54, 96
ABAB lyric pattern, 44–45
Armstrong, Louis, 34, 48

B

Banjo, *16*, 17–18, 31, 47, 79
Basie, William "Count," 70–71
Beatles, 99–101
Billboard (magazine), 52
Blue notes, 18, 47
Blues
    Chicago blues, 99
    city blues, 38, 85–87
    classic blues, 38, 61–63, 66, 69, 79
    commercialization, 36–37
    country blues, 30, 36, 38, 65–66, 80,
      85–86
    dancing and, 36, 43, 52, 89
    defined, 10–11
    Delta blues, 82, 87, 89, 92
    development, 23–28
    effect on US culture, 46–47
    emotion, 10, 21, 29, 32, 69
    folk blues, 30
    jump blues, 52
    lyric patterns, 31, 44–45, 53–54, 96
    modern blues, 30, 69, 89
    optimism and, 11, 85
    oral history, 34–35
    overview, 10–12
    slavery and, 9, 11
    twelve-bar blues structure, 30, 34, 35–
      36, 52, 57, 58, 90
    See also White blues; Female blues art-
      ists; Male blues artists
Bo Diddley, 100
Bonamassa, Joe, 104
Bradford, Perry, 38
Brenston, Jackie, 59
Broonzy, Lee Conley "Big Bill," *86*
    blues style, 85–86
    development of blues and, 42
    influence, 100
    life, 84–85
    Memphis Minnie and, 67–68, 97

C

Call and response, 20–21, 49–50, 52
Carter, A.P., 96
Cash, Johnny, 98, 106
Charles, Ray, *55*, 56
Clapton, Eric, 48, 93, 101–105, *103*
Cole, Nat King, 52
Common (artist), 60
Cotton Club, 73
Country and western music, 57–59, 96–97
Crudup, Arthur "Big Boy," 59, 97

D

Dancing
    blues and, 36, 43, 52, 89
    church music and, 21
    slaves and, *16*, 17, 18
    variety shows and, 22

PICTURE CREDITS

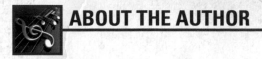

Michael V. Uschan has written eighty-nine books including *Life of an American Soldier in Iraq*, for which he won the 2005 Council for Wisconsin Writers Juvenile Nonfiction Award. Uschan began his career as a writer and editor with United Press International, a wire service that provided stories to newspapers, radio, and television. Journalism is sometimes called "history in a hurry"; Uschan considers writing history books a natural extension of the skills he developed in his many years as a journalist. He and his wife Barbara reside in the Milwaukee suburb of Franklin, Wisconsin.